Auntie Aisha Answers

Auntie Aisha Answers

The Muslim Tween's Ultimate Guide to Growing Up

Aisha Hussain Rasheed

Auntie Aisha Answers
The Muslim Tween's Ultimate Guide to Growing Up

All Rights Reserved © 2024 by Daybreak Press

No part of this book may be reproduced or transmitted in any form or by any means, graphic, electronic or mechanical, including photocopying, recording, typing, or by any information storage retrieval system, without the permission of the publisher.

Published by Daybreak Press
3533 Lexington Avenue North | Arden Hills, MN 55126
www.rabata.org/daybreakpress | daybreakpress@rabata.org

ISBN (Print): 978-1-7345914-6-0
ISBN (Ebook): 978-1-7345914-7-7
LCCN: 2024937103

Illustrator/Cover art: Magdalena Zaręba | artstation.com/mebhe
Cover design: Hagar Diab | hagardiab.com
Design and typesetting: Islam Farid | Islamfarid.net

Printed in the United States of America

Contents

Looking for Answers 1

Little Bodies, Big Questions   3

(1) Every Body Is a Blessing 5
(2) My Disabled Body 9
(3) Every Male and Female Body 19
(4) Everybody Deserves Privacy 25
(5) Everybody Deserves Care 29
(6) Everybody Deserves Autonomy 47
(7) Everybody Needs Healing 51

Growing Pains   55

(8) Everybody Grows Up 57
(9) Everybody Has a Role to Play 77
(10) Everybody Must Go Back 87

Endnotes & Additional Resources 93

Looking for Answers

Being a kid is hard work. I know. Because I used to be a kid too. I had so many questions that I wanted answers to, but I was worried it wasn't right to ask. So I had to look for many answers by myself. At first, I didn't know where to look. I had to become a full-on sleuth and find people who could tell me where to look for answers to all of my

1,309,479 questions.

In this book, you will find answers to questions about **you**. You might have had questions about your body, for example. Or your mind. Or your spirit. You might also have wondered about how you're changing as you become older. We will try to figure out at least some of these things so you can be confident about yourself and about growing up.

I also want to share with you where to look for answers when you need them, because one of the things I learned growing up is that having questions is a good thing and searching for answers is not as hard as I thought.

When we have questions about Islam, the right place to look for answers is in the Qur'an and the teachings of the Prophet Muḥammad *ṣallallāhu ʿalaihi wa sallam* (may the peace and blessings of Allah be upon him). Of course, we will need help from teachers who can explain the answers to us as well. So at the very end of this book, I've also written notes about where I found answers to some of my questions about Islam. That way next time you have a question, you will know where to begin looking for answers too.

You will notice this book discusses certain things about some of our body parts. These things are important to know so you can be prepared for the changes that may happen to your body as you grow older. You will notice that many people refer to some body parts with "euphemisms," or slang terms. We won't be doing that in this book. We will use the anatomically correct terms for your body parts here. Your eyes are your eyes—not "the windows to your soul." Your tongue is your tongue. Your arm is your arm. And that applies to all your body parts.

Some of the things we talk about in this book might be things you already know. But I thought I'll mention them anyway, because, when something is important, it helps to be reminded of it once in a while.

There will be some new information for you in this book as well *inshā' Allāh* (with Allah's Permission) that will hopefully answer, or at least provide clues to, any questions you may still have. If you need any help understanding what I've written, please ask a grown-up like your parents or a teacher.

Speaking of parents, whenever I suggest that you ask your parents, I mean any one of your caregivers. They are the ones who care for you, provide for you, nurture you, and help you be a better person. We know that all families aren't the same. For some of us, the people who are caring for us are not necessarily our biological parents. Still, they love and care for us and try their best to help us face life's challenges.

May Allah love and reward all the grown-ups who love and support us. *Āmīn!*

Happy investigating, my brilliant sleuths!

Little Bodies, Big Questions

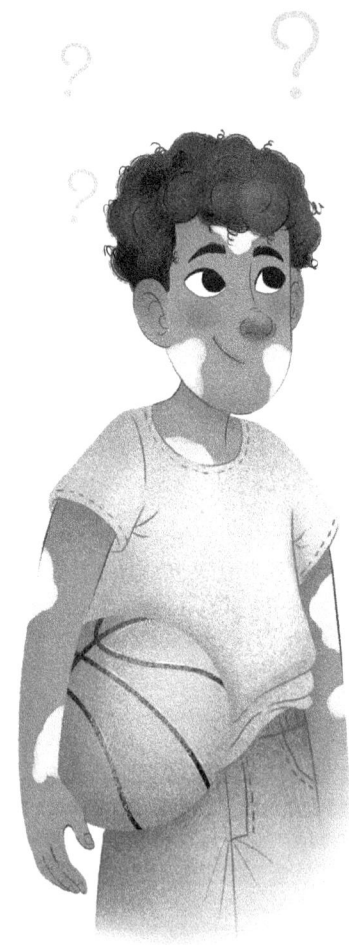

(1)
Every Body Is a Blessing

Your parents have probably already told you this, but I want to tell you this again in case you've forgotten. Everything we have is a blessing from Allah. The air we breathe; the food we eat; the water we drink; trees, mountains, clouds; everything in our lives; and even the fact that we are alive is a blessing from Allah *subḥānahu wa taʿālā*.

Today, I want you to think about one specific blessing Allah has given us:

If you stand in front of a mirror, you'll see that some parts of your body are exposed. Your face almost definitely is. That is, unless you like to read books wearing your mask. Maybe your arms and legs are enjoying some fresh air too. Other parts of your body are covered by clothes. Your thighs. Your chest. Your belly.

Some parts of your body, like your hair, are on the outside. Others, like your internal organs, are on the inside. Our most important internal organs are protected by our skeleton—our skull and spine house our brain and spinal cord, and our ribcage makes sure our lungs and heart don't fall out and run away 😂. Our skeleton is covered with flesh and skin, which makes sure we are protected from dangerous elements in the environment. You've probably learned this in science class, haven't you?

Look at yourself again. Closely this time.

Draw a picture of yourself here. Make a list of the things you like most about your body and about yourself.

Everything in your body is a blessing from Allah. Every part has a function. Every single part of our body has a job to do.

Do you sometimes compare your body to your siblings' bodies or your friends' bodies? Isn't it amazing how many different shapes and sizes we all come in?

Some of us are tall. Some of us are short. Some of us are smaller. Some of us are bigger. Some of us have light skin. Some of us have dark skin. Some of us have moles or freckles. Some of us don't. A few of us may even have four fingers or six toes. Most of these differences don't change how our bodies work. But sometimes, parts of our body might not function the way they do in other people's bodies. Sometimes it's something we are born with. The big word for that is a **congenital condition.** Other times, it's because of an illness or accident that happens after we are born.

Some of us have legs that can't carry them. They use crutches or wheelchairs to move around. Others have eyes that don't see very well. They wear glasses to help them see better. If they can't see at all, they might use a service dog or a cane to figure out where they're going, and they might learn new information by listening to audiobooks or reading books that use a special type of writing called **Braille.** Some people's ears don't hear very well. They may need to use hearing aids or they may use sign language.

Whatever these disabilities may be, we should always work hard to make sure that everyone is able to go to parks, schools, offices, and mosques. Go everywhere, really. Do public places where you live have ramps so people who use crutches and wheelchairs can get around there easily? Everyone should also be able to read and listen to important information. Do you think the books you read are also available in Braille or in audio format? Do the TV shows and news broadcasts in your country have subtitles or sign language interpretation?

We will be talking a little more about this going forward. For now, I just want you to know this: No matter what differences we have in our bodies, our bodies are always blessings from Allah. And we are all beautiful creations of Allah. Allah is *al-Khāliq*, the Creator who created us. Allah is *al-Muṣawwir*, the Designer who designed us. Allah is *al-Badīʿ*, the Creator who created us uniquely without any previous examples.[1]

Alḥamdulillāh. Thank God.

(2)
My Disabled Body

You may have a body that works differently from everybody else's. (This is also for everyone who has a sibling or friend whose body works differently than the way most others' do.)

I know I've already said that all bodies are blessings: The short and the tall, the small and the big. But I want to tell you this again. *Your body is a blessing*. I am telling you this again, because I realize that when your body works differently from others', it can be exhausting and frustrating.

A lot of times, being different feels troublesome. Everyone else who doesn't have the type of body that you have doesn't seem to understand how your body works. Architects might not think of making buildings you can go into easily. Authors might not think of making audiobooks you can listen to. Classmates might just keep on talking to everyone else even though you can't hear them. You know you could understand if they made an effort. But they don't—maybe they don't know how. And that can make you feel left out.

I am so sorry about that!

What I'm going to tell you now is something sad and **downright wrong**. But we have to know the sad and wrong things that happen around us so that we can correct them, right? Sometimes people who don't have the same challenges that you do aren't aware of how hard it can be to navigate through a world that isn't built with you in mind. Other times, the kind of technology and devices that are needed to help us when we have differences in our bodies may not have been developed yet.

Don't let that bring you down, though. There are many people around the world who know that this is unfair. And, as all good people do when they see something wrong, they are working hard to make things right. There are brilliant scientists and inventors inventing amazing tools to help people with different bodies do everything they need to do without feeling limited. Many of these brilliant people themselves have disabled bodies, so they know from experience what kind of tools are helpful.

In some places, there are group meetings and playdates for people who have similar conditions in their bodies so they can become friends, play together, and share their stories and experiences with each other. It can be helpful to have friends with similar experiences.

Now, there are differences in our bodies that can be seen. Most of the time, though, the differences in the way our bodies work cannot be seen easily by an outsider. Do you, or anyone you know, have an invisible thing that makes your body, or their body, work differently?

What are some parts of our body that aren't easily seen? I think our brain might be a good example. When our body receives information through our senses, our brain is the computer that sorts through all that information and figures out what it means. What if someone's brain worked differently from other people's brains from the moment they were born? What if someone had a terrible fall or accident that hurt their head so badly that it injured their brain? Would that make a difference in how they are able to deal with the world around them? I think it might.

Think about our hearts or our lungs. If these organs work differently in someone's body, we can't necessarily see it either. But don't you think it would make a huge difference in their life? Yes, I think so too.

If I can't learn things the same way my friends do, does that mean I'm not as smart as they are?

Some of us learn better through books. Others learn best if they listen to someone or watch a video. These are different learning styles. We each have our own unique style of learning.

For some of us, though, none of the learning styles that our friends use seem to work at all. It may be that you haven't managed to find your unique learning style. Or it might mean that you have different educational needs altogether.

Some disabilities can also make it difficult for us to play and interact with our friends. It might be because we have trouble figuring out something called "social cues." Social cues are basically little hints that people give in the way they behave or in the tone of their voice to help express what they mean. Some of us with disabilities might have trouble noticing these hints or figuring out what they mean, so it could become a little harder to interact with our friends.

I hope that you will always remember that having some learning difficulties or special educational needs does not mean you're not as smart as your friends are. It just means that your kind of smart is different from theirs.

It's important for us to share with our parents and teachers if we think we're having trouble with learning. They can take us to see a doctor or run some tests to help us figure out if we have any special educational needs. Then they'll be able to recommend tools and strategies that match our learning needs. They may give us some medication to treat the symptoms of our condition. They may suggest we be given a little more time to take a test than others. In some cases, they can enroll us in our own special class with a specially trained teacher who can help figure out unique learning techniques that will work for us.

No matter what you do to deal with your disability, remember that this is your personal journey. Other than your parents or guardians and teachers, you really don't have to tell anyone about your condition. Sometimes people might be curious about it, though, and ask you questions. You don't have to answer if you aren't comfortable.

If you feel like you want to answer questions about your condition, it could help to have prepared a short answer ahead of time. How about you say something like this:

"Thank you for asking me nicely. I have a condition called

_____

That means my body might work a little differently than yours does.

It _____

_____

But why did Allah give you this body and not a "normal" body like everybody else has? Why can't we all have bodies that work exactly the same?

Firstly, I hope you never look at yourself and think that you are "not normal" or that you are "weird." You are exactly the way Allah designed you to be. *Allāhu akbar*!!!

Second, the fact that we are not all the same actually makes us stronger together. That is *if* we respect and embrace ourselves and each other with all our differences.

I want to introduce you to a beautiful word that describes this sentiment:

diversity

Diversity describes what makes each and every one of us unique and special. If you think about it, it's kind of like planet Earth. Deserts, tropical forests, grasslands, islands, mountains, wetlands, and oceans all come together to make up this beautiful planet of ours. Deserts can't grow trees like forests do. Tropical forests don't have snow like mountaintops do. Wetlands don't have beautiful corals like oceans do. But they are all important and beautiful. And without this diversity, our Earth could not survive.

Even within each one of these habitats, there are many different species of plants and animals. Each species has its own unique strengths and weaknesses. Each species is important. And every single one of them helps make their habitat a healthy one.

And just like our beautiful Earth and all its wonderful habitats, without all the unique and different people in the world respecting and helping each other, we would not be able to survive either.

When you think about it, this applies to all of us, regardless of whether we have disabilities or not.

Imagine you live in a specific habitat.

Now pick a plant or animal in that habitat that you think may be a lot like you. What are its weaknesses? What are some challenges it faces because of them? What are its greatest strengths? How does it help keep its habitat a healthy one?

I'll go first.

If my habitat were a woodland, I think I'd be a mosquito.

Its greatest weakness is that it can't communicate or explain itself well. Because of this, many people misunderstand mosquitoes. Its greatest strength is that it can fly and use its proboscis to get food from all types of places. Mosquitos don't just get their food from animals and people; some mosquitoes get their food from flowers. This helps pollinate plants. People may not realize it, but mosquitoes help keep the environment healthy and green.

Now, you try.

If my habitat were a _____, I think I'd be a _____.
Its greatest weakness is _____
Because of this _____. Its greatest strength is _____
It can use it to _____.
People may not realize it, but _____ help keep the environment healthy and colorful.

Also, remember that our life here in this world is temporary. That means it will not last forever. It will end. The real life, the real world, is in the *Ākhirah*, the Hereafter. We can't see it now. We can't even imagine it properly with all its wonder.

In this temporary world, Allah gave all of us different types of tests and trials. If you look at all the blessings you have in this world, they are also a kind of test. You have to use your blessings in a way that will please Allah. That is the purpose and privilege of our lives.

When we do things that please Allah, our souls and spirits feel good. Our soul is the part of us that is not our body and leaves our body when we die. So when we pray, fast, are kind to one another, remind each other to be good, and help one another, our souls feel better and get stronger.

Let's think of it like playing a video game. Doing good deeds to please Allah is like completing **missions**. The more missions you complete, the more points you get. When you fail missions, you lose points. And if you do extra missions, you can even get extra points. And when we put our best effort into being the best version of ourselves, Allah will, through His *love* and *mercy*, forgive our mistakes and accept us into Jannah, *inshā' Allāh*.

May Allah give us the chance to do extra missions and get extra points. *Āmīn*!

Allah does not expect you to do things your body is not able to do.[2] If you can't bend down for *rukūʿ* and *sujūd* in prayer because your body doesn't work that way, you can just do what you're able to. Allah will accept your prayer and reward you. If you can't recite Qur'an because you can't hear the words, you can learn the meaning in sign language and think of that meaning in your prayers. If you have a condition that makes it truly impossible for you to stay still, Allah will accept your prayer even though you were fidgeting. If you can't fast because you have to take medicine during the day, Allah does not want you to fast; He wants you to take care of your health while doing other acts of worship and observing *dhikr* instead. And all the while, Allah will reward you for your patience.

If you have a family member who does not understand the world around them, know that Allah will not be angry at them at all and will straightaway accept them into Jannah. Allah is *al-Raḥmān, al-Raḥīm*—the Most Merciful in giving blessings to everyone, and especially in granting blessings to those who believe and ask for mercy and blessings.

You know that the people who met the Prophet *ṣallallāhu ʿalaihi wa sallam* and believed in his message are called his companions, right? There was a lady among his companions called **Ummu Zufar**. She was a tall, Black woman. She had an illness called epilepsy. It was an illness in her brain and nervous system that made her have seizures. When she had seizures, she would lose control of her body and her body would shake and spasm uncontrollably. She tried all the treatments that were available at that time for her illness, but none of them worked. She still had seizures. Sometimes, she even had seizures in the mosque when she was there. She felt very **distressed**.

One day, she came to the Prophet *ṣallallāhu 'alaihi wa sallam,* told him about her illness, and asked him to please make *du'ā* for Allah to heal her. The Prophet *ṣallallāhu 'alaihi wa sallam* said to her, "If you choose, you can patiently endure your illness in this world, and you will go to Jannah. Or, if you want me to, I will pray to Allah to end this illness for you." She said, "I will **patiently** go through this illness." Then she thought a little and said, "But when I have seizures, sometimes my *'awrah* gets uncovered in public. Will you please pray to Allah to prevent that from happening?" And the Prophet *ṣallallāhu 'alaihi wa sallam* prayed for her.

Other companions who were there that day and knew her story respected her very much and taught their students to respect her. After all, **she was a person of Jannah**.[3]

Sometimes, you may still feel low, though, and that's okay. Those feelings are part of what make us human. They are meant to help us have **empathy** for people who have things harder than we do. When they come, just acknowledge them and ask Allah for the strength of spirit to get through them. Ask Allah to make you a better Muslim and a better human being because of them.

If you feel like crying, have a good cry. If you need a hug, ask for a hug. Ask for help when you need to. The people who love you will try to help you as best they can, because true love and true friendship means **respecting** and **valuing** each other's differences, supporting one another with care, and bonding over the things we share.

(3)
Every Male and Female Body

All living things that Allah created in this world can **reproduce**. This means that Allah gave them the ability to multiply, or make babies.

Some living things, like bacteria, divide into two exact copies. Others have little spores that spread and become grown-ups. In many plants, you can take a cutting from the grown-up plant, plant it or put it in water to grow roots, and it will become a plant of its own. These types of reproduction are called "asexual reproduction." One adult by itself becomes the "parent" and has the ability to make more of itself.

But in many plants, most animals, and for us humans, that is not how reproduction happens. You can't divide and become two exact copies of yourself. You don't spread spores that grow into other humans. And I'm sure I can't take a "cutting" from you and grow another you, either. Or would you be okay with "lending me a hand" so we can do an experiment? 😃

The kind of reproduction that happens in us is called "sexual reproduction." That means that one cell from a female and one cell from a male come together to grow into a baby.

Some creatures, like birds and reptiles, have babies by laying eggs. The baby will develop inside the egg until it is ready to hatch. Have you ever seen an egg hatch? Who would have thought something so fascinating and amazing could also be so slimy and gross?!

In other creatures, called mammals, babies develop through different stages inside their mother's tummy, in an organ called "the uterus" or "the womb." The time the baby takes to develop inside the mother's uterus is called the "gestation period." And when a mom is carrying a developing baby inside her, we say that she is "pregnant." In humans, this takes about **forty weeks**. When the gestation period is over, the baby needs to be out in the world to grow further. So at that point, the mom is able to push the baby out. That is how our mothers give birth to us.

Being pregnant and giving birth is hard and exhausting. It can also be painful. That is part of the reason why in Islam we are told to be kind to our parents,[4] especially our moms.[5]

Anyway, in order for sexual reproduction to happen, there need to be two individuals of different sexes: male and female.

Male and female bodies are different in their respective reproductive systems. The reproductive system is the group of organs that help us reproduce, or make babies. In the male body, the reproductive system is made up of the penis, the testicles, and the prostate gland. The penis and the scrotum (that's the "bag" of skin right under the penis that holds and protects the testicles) are visible from the outside of a male's body.

In the female body, the reproductive system consists of the vulva, the vagina, and the uterus (or the womb). There are also two fallopian tubes and two ovaries, one on each side of the uterus. The vulva are visible on the outside, but the rest of the female reproductive system is inside the lower part of a female's belly.

Allah has created our reproductive system in an amazing way. From the beginning of **puberty**, the testicles in a male body start to produce a type of cell called "sperm cells." In the female body, the ovaries start producing a cell called an "ovum," which is also called an "egg cell." (Can you believe that it's not only birds and reptiles that come from eggs? We were once eggs too!) Anyway, when a sperm cell and an egg cell are able to come together, they combine and start to multiply until a whole baby is formed inside the uterus. *Subḥānallāh*!

These are the differences between the male and female sexes that we can see in our organs. There are also differences in our genes that determine whether we are male or female.

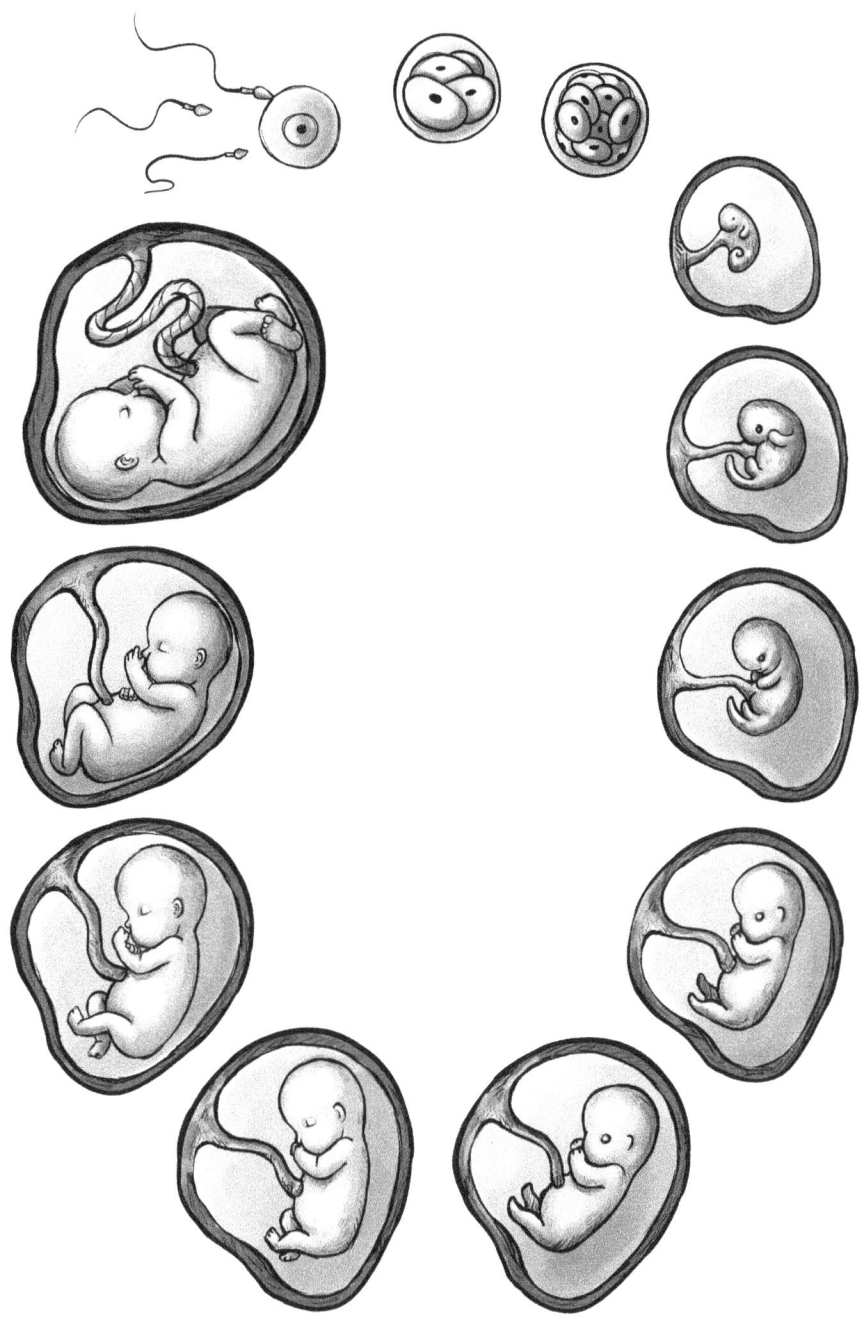

Genes—which are different from **jeans**, by the way, because we don't wear them 😄—are the blueprints inside our cells that determine what features and traits we have. They are woven together into very tiny little structures called "chromosomes." In most of us, the nucleus of every single one of our cells contains twenty-three pairs of chromosomes (or forty-six chromosomes altogether). We call one pair of these chromosomes the sex chromosomes. If one of us is male, he will have XY chromosomes in *all* of the 30 or so **trillion** cells in his body! On the other hand, if one of us is female, she will have XX chromosomes in all of the 30 or so trillion cells in *her* body!!

Allah has also created a few of us who don't have clearly male or female features. Such people are referred to as being **intersex**. If we are intersex, we might not have clearly male or clearly female reproductive organs. We might have a mixture of male and female features. Or we might have an extra or a missing sex chromosome in our genes.

These details are private, of course. So unless someone shares their personal information with you, it wouldn't be polite to assume or ask details about them. And, if you happen to be intersex, you don't have to share that information except with those who have to know (like your guardians and your doctors) or those who you'd like to know.

Always remember that whether you are male, female, or intersex does not make you any more or less important or valuable than anyone else. We are all equally **human**. We are all equally **important**. We are all equally loved and blessed by Allah. And we all have equal responsibility to follow Allah's commands and try to be **good people**.[6]

Most **rules** and **responsibilities** in Islam apply in the same way to men and women. But there are a few rules and responsibilities in Islam that are assigned only to one sex or the other.

For example, during salah and when in public in front of men who are not part of their close family, grown-up Muslim women have the honorable responsibility of *covering* most of their bodies, including their hair.

On the other hand, when a man and a woman get married, the groom has the honorable responsibility of giving his bride a bridal gift and **spending** for the family's home, food, and clothes. Allah rewards them for carrying out these responsibilities properly.

If we are intersex, we are normally advised to follow the rules that apply to people of the sex that we're most similar to. Of course, there will be more details that we will have to learn based on our individual condition. Ask a grown-up to help you learn these details and practice accordingly. Remember: When we don't know something, asking questions to learn more is the right thing to do.

(4)
Everybody Deserves Privacy

Do you remember when you were a baby? What a silly question! Of course you don't! None of us do!

What I meant to ask was, do you have photographs of when you were a little baby? Do you notice that in some of them, you're just wearing your diapers (or are they called nappies where you're from)? Maybe you have photos from when you were a toddler where you were only wearing undies too. Some of us may even have photos of us wearing nothing at all, and our bum is showing. How silly! We were all such cute babies though, weren't we?

I bet you wouldn't want to take a photo of yourself in your undies now though, right? In fact, you might not even want to show those baby pictures to your friends. You might not want your parents to show them to their friends, either. It's **awkward** and **embarrassing**!

It's perfectly natural to feel this way. If you have photos like that, and you don't want your parents to show other people, remember to tell them how you feel and ask them to keep those photos private. *Inshā' Allāh* they will respect your feelings and do as you ask.

As we grow older, we don't like to take our clothes off in front of other people. We just don't want other people to be able to see our private parts.

Is your **face** a "private part" that you don't want anyone else to see? No. Your **hands**? No.

Then what is a private part? Our buttocks and our genitals are definitely private parts, right? We don't show those parts to other people. But remember, even those parts of our body are beautifully created by Allah to carry out their function. We don't cover them because they are ugly or bad. We cover them simply because they are **private** .[7]

Our private parts are part of our **'awrah**. As we grow older, we start to cover more parts of our body. You probably already cover more than just your genitals and your buttocks. Like your thighs. And your chest. And your tummy. And when we are in public, we cover our bodies a bit more than we do when we are at home with just our family.

According to Islamic rules, grown-up women have to cover most of their bodies when they are in public and when they perform salah. Grown-up men have to cover up at least from their belly buttons all the way down to their knees.

> I'm sure you see Muslim grown-ups around you following those rules, or doing their best to follow them. (After all, even grown-ups have trouble following the rules properly sometimes. It's true!) I'm sure you will learn more about these rules as you grow older, and we will discuss them later in the book too.

Covering ourselves up and **treasuring** our privacy is one of the ways we show respect for the body Allah has blessed us with.

> You will notice also that there might be differences in the way people dress or style their hair or do things based on their sex. These things tend to change from place to place. They could also change in any particular community as time passes. It's always important that we respect others who may dress differently than we do, for example, while remaining true to our own values and principles.

And just like we would want other people to respect our privacy, we should respect their privacy too. If one of our friends wants to change their clothes, we should let them have the room and close the door behind us. We can come back and play together after they've changed.

We should also remember to **knock** and ask permission before we enter a room. Even in our own home. And if we go to visit our friends, we should always ring the doorbell and wait to be let in. This is enough if we live in a big city.

But if we live in a village or a small town where the windows are often left open and we can hear the people inside, we can try saying **salām** up to three times. But if they're still busy and not able to come to the door, we should understand that it's probably not a good time for visiting.[8] We can come back to visit another time.

"Assalamu alaikum" is a short phrase that means a lot of things. It means "I don't want to harm you. I am peaceful toward you. I pray Allah gives you peace."

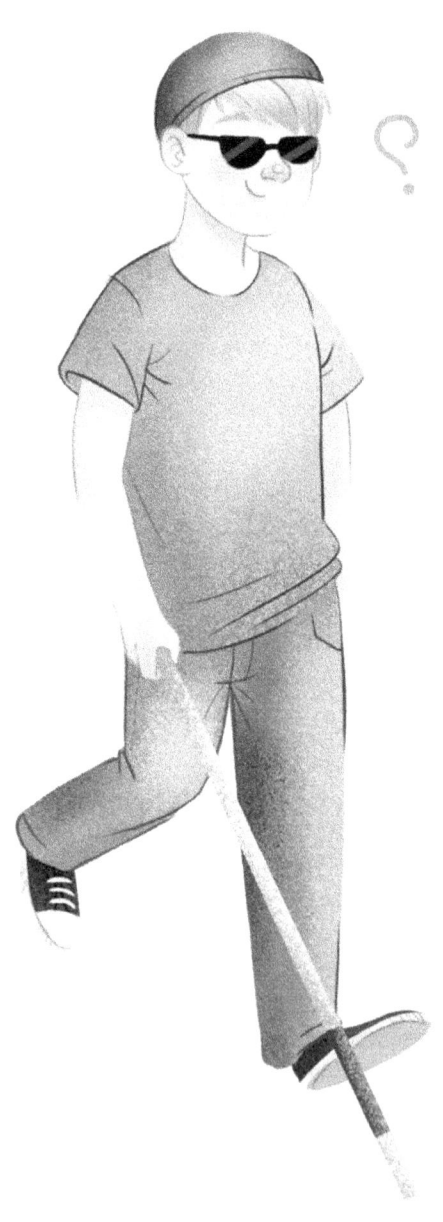

(5)
Everybody Deserves Care

We've already talked about privacy as one of the ways we respect the bodies Allah *subḥānahu wa taʿālā* blessed us with. But that's not the only way we can respect our bodies and be **grateful** to Allah, *al-Khāliq*, for creating them for us.

Another very important way for us to respect our bodies and show our gratitude for them is by taking proper **care** of them.

Think about it. Imagine there was a very cool toy or device you wanted to have. It can be a video game. A Lego set. A board game. A jigsaw puzzle. A set of paint and brushes for your artwork. Hot Wheels cars. Anything you like. Now, imagine your parents got it for you. It can be a brand new one from the shop or, even better, it can be a toy that someone else before you had loved and played with and has since outgrown. Your parents or someone else who loves you very much got you that toy as a gift.

After you open it up and use it or play with it, are you just going to throw it on the floor and leave it there? Are you going to just ignore it as people step on it and break it, or even hurt themselves tripping over it? Would that be a good way to show your appreciation to the person who gave you such a brilliant gift?

It's much better to play with your toy and then put it away somewhere safe. When you do that, your parents will also know that you're being responsible and taking care of your things. *Bārakallāhu fīk*! May Allah bless you!

Well, just like you're supposed to take care of all the other things Allah has entrusted you with, you are also supposed to take care of your own self.

That includes **taking care of your spirit** through prayer and good deeds to please Allah. Another way you take care of your spirit is by not doing bad things, like telling lies, cheating, and hurting people. Allah created us to do good things, so when we do the opposite, our spirits become tired and weighed down. In the Qur'an, Allah describes our spirits as getting stained or rusted when we do things that make Him unhappy with us.[9]

Let's think about that for a while. It's kind of like our soul is a beautiful, clean piece of cloth. Every time we do something that will make Allah unhappy with us, a stain marks the cloth. Imagine if we keep doing things like that repeatedly. The cloth will get stained over and over again. The original color of the cloth won't be visible at all. Neither will the beautiful pattern that was on it.

But we all make mistakes. Does that mean we are stained forever and can never be beautiful and good again?! Of course not. Remember how loving our parents are with us? If they are ever upset with us because of a mistake we made, what are we supposed to do? We accept our mistake, ask them to forgive us, and try to do better. Correct? Do they stay upset with us forever? No. Our parents love us. They wouldn't even think of being upset with us forever! Well, Allah is even more loving and more merciful than our parents.[10] Allah promised us that if we sincerely ask forgiveness for our mistakes, He will forgive us. Allah is *al-'Afuww*, the Forgiver.

This doesn't only mean that Allah forgives us, though. This means He also removes all the stains our mistakes have put on our soul! It's almost as if we didn't make the mistake in the first place—except that we remember the lessons we learned from our mistake. And Allah is so merciful, we can go back to Him and ask for forgiveness all the time. That includes when we slip up and make the same mistake twice. Or three times. As long as you really, really, REALLY are sorry and mean to not make the mistake again, Allah does not get tired of you seeking forgiveness. So we shouldn't get tired of trying to be better. And we absolutely must not give up on ourselves... even if we slip up.

We know that our spirits and souls feel hurt when we commit sins. But sometimes, if we do something sinful very often, it becomes one of our habits. We might even start to enjoy doing it or be anxious when we don't do it.

For example, if someone tells lies very often, lying can become second nature to them. They might tell lies very easily, without even thinking about it. How do we make sure this doesn't happen to us?!

Reciting **adhkār** is a brilliant way for us to keep our actions pleasing to Allah. It reminds us that Allah is with us. He is watching us, watching over us, and protecting us.

Taking care of yourself also includes making sure you get the information and thinking skills you're going to need in the future. One of the ways we get this knowledge is through our school lessons. But we also get a lot of this knowledge throughout our lives from our family and friends, and sometimes even from strangers. **We never really stop learning.**

Self-care also means being mindful of your **emotions**. And the first step for us to do that is to learn about them.

Remember this: **no emotion is bad**. Some emotions can be uncomfortable, but that doesn't mean you shouldn't have them. Emotions are simply how we feel about the things that are happening around us.

When happy things happen, we feel happy. When we are looking forward to something fun, we feel excited. In exactly the same way, when uncomfortable things happen, we feel uncomfortable. Sad things make us feel sad. If things don't go the way we were hoping they would go, we might feel frustrated. If we are preparing for a big exam or competition, we might feel nervous or even slightly **anxious**.

What are some uncomfortable emotions you might need help dealing with? How can you make sure you're taking charge of your big emotions and calmly dealing with them? Who can you ask for help?

One way to manage big emotions is to try taking a few deep belly breaths.

To do this, first get comfortable. If you're standing up, find a comfortable place to sit down. Close your eyes. Take a deep breath with your nose. Feel the air going through your nose and filling up your chest. Feel the air in your belly and hold it in. Then slowly, let the air out through your mouth.

You can also try singing a song or saying some of your *adhkār*. Running or jumping a little might help too. These are just my suggestions. You can find your own little tricks to help you calm down or handle big emotions when they come.

When we understand our emotions, they can also help guide how we act in different situations. For example, when we have a big competition coming up, we may feel nervous. Our nervousness is a signal for us that we have to do our best to prepare for the big competition. If we understand that, then we are likely to attend trainings and practices so that we can perform our best in the competition. If we don't understand that, we might end up putting off practice because of how nervous we feel. Then we might not be prepared at all when the competition comes around.

We might also feel a little anxious or embarrassed to try something new. What if I hurt myself? What if I am terrible at it? Oh my God! What if I make an absolute fool of myself?!

These feelings are very normal. Everyone feels them. But we shouldn't let them stop us from enjoying ourselves and having new experiences with our friends and loved ones! Something that helped me was facing my fear slowly. Let me tell you something I did.

When I first learned to swim, I was very scared of swimming in deep water. My home is on a beautiful island, and the island is surrounded by beautiful coral reefs. My brothers were good swimmers. They had been swimming and snorkeling and diving for a long time. And they told me about all the wonderful fish and colorful coral. I wanted to see all the magnificent things they talked about, but I was afraid to swim above the coral reef because the water is deep there.

So my brothers and I came up with a brilliant plan. Every time we went to the beach together, I would swim just a little deeper than the time before. My brothers stayed with me, and if I got too scared, they would quickly help me swim back to shore.

Every time we went to the beach, I was becoming a better swimmer. Sometimes, I would even see an odd parrotfish pecking at a coral. Slowly, I was able to swim deep enough to see a lot more of the coral reef. I could see brain corals and table corals and staghorn corals and sea fans. I could see parrotfish and unicorn fish and surgeonfish. I even saw an eagle ray swimming once! It looked like it was flying in the water! *Alḥamdulillāh* I was able to conquer my fear of swimming in the deep. It is awesome!!

Another emotion we might feel is frustration. When we're frustrated, it could mean that the way we've been doing things isn't getting us the results we were hoping for. When we understand this, it helps us try doing things a bit differently. Maybe we could even get help from someone else.

> Sometimes, we might have started an activity or tried to learn a new sport and found out that we can't quite figure out how to do it no matter how hard we try. That might be the reason why we are feeling frustrated. Sometimes, it might help to simply accept that we just aren't able to do this one thing we were trying to do. That's okay. After all, we are human. We all have our own talents, but we don't have to be able to do *everything*.
>
> It can help to discuss things with our parents, teachers, or friends and other adults who love and care for us to decide if we should stop trying what we are trying to do. I think it's also important that we don't make a decision when we're in the middle of feeling frustrated. Take a break for a while. When you're feeling calmer and more relaxed, have a think whether you want to keep on trying or move on to a new activity or sport.
>
> No matter what you decide, don't feel disappointed in yourself. The good news is that even if we aren't good at doing everything, our family and friends will always love us. And most importantly, Allah loves us.

Remember: Just like we share our happiness and joy and excitement with the people we love, we should share our sadness and worries and frustrations with them too. Our feelings of happiness grow when we share our joy with loved ones. But when we share sadness and worries with people we love, those emotions can shrink. What an amazing **miracle!**

Sometimes you may not feel ready to share your feelings with the people you love. It may be that you haven't fully understood your feelings yet. Or you don't think the people you love can fully understand how you're feeling. In those situations, it can help to write down your thoughts in a **notebook** or **journal** or record them on **voice notes**. Or maybe you're better at expressing yourself through doodles, drawings, or paintings. There may even be times when you could talk to a school counselor or therapist about your feelings. All of these are healthy ways to figure out and express your emotions.

And remember, you can always, *always* **share how you feel with Allah** subḥānahu wa taʿālā in your duʿā. He is never tired of listening to us sharing with Him.

One way that you can take good care of yourself and your emotions is to **set up clear boundaries**. Boundaries are basically rules you follow for yourself when dealing with other people, and that you ask them to follow also. For example, we talked about privacy earlier. Your privacy is a boundary that people should respect.

What are some other healthy boundaries?

One of my healthy boundaries has to do with books. I absolutely love reading, and I keep a lot of books. Sometimes I like to let my friends borrow them too. I just ask them to follow some simple rules.

> If you'd like to borrow a book from me, please ask me first. I will give it to you if I can. When you borrow it, please take proper care of it. Please make sure my book doesn't get wet or torn, for example. And ABSOLUTELY NEVER EVER fold the page corners. And finally, once you have read the book, please make sure you give it back to me.
>
> Thank you

If my friends don't respect my books, it makes me very sad. It shows me they don't respect my boundaries. I will probably explain my boundaries more clearly to them if they ignore my book boundaries once. But if they keep doing it, I cannot let them borrow my books anymore.

Another boundary I have is that I ask all my friends and family members to respect my values and my feelings. We don't always have to agree about everything with our friends and family. We might disagree about our favorite foods. My friend might have a completely different sense of fashion from me. We might feel differently about all kinds of things. I love bugs and creepy-crawlies, but many of my family members think they are gross and, well, creepy. And that's okay. We don't have to agree. People who love each other can even disagree about how they should live their lives. Some of your friends or family members may even have a different religion than you. Everyone has the right to have their own opinion.

I try to be a good friend and good family member to all my loved ones, and I try not to put them in situations where they may be scared or uncomfortable (asking them to hold my pet *TARANTULA*, for example!). Although I think tarantulas are cool, I respect their feelings. 🕷

Similarly, if my friend is a vegetarian, I would never try to trick her into eating meat. If my friend is scared of heights, I wouldn't play a prank on him that involves heights.

I want my friends to do the same for me. I want them to respect my principles and help me to follow them. I'd like them to respect my feelings and try to understand them. I think that is a healthy boundary to have.

You don't have to spend your precious time in places where people are purposely being unkind to you or others. If anyone makes fun of others or hurts others, that is not a good place for you to be. That is not the kind of "fun" that you should try to be part of.

Instead, spend time with friends who *love* and *support* each other to do good things and be better versions of themselves. And if you see someone being treated badly, try to help that person. Stick up for them or, if you need to, get a grown-up to help.

Remember: Just like you need care, love, and respect, everyone around you needs them too. So you will have to treat your friends and loved ones with love and care as well. And you have to **respect** everyone else's boundaries. By doing this, you're showing respect for others and showing everyone around you how you want to be treated. You're also expressing gratitude to the people who treat you with love and respect.

Always remember: Everyone has their own experiences and emotions that they are trying to deal with in their lives. We might not be able to know exactly how they feel, but we can remember that everyone has struggles we don't know about and we can try to have empathy for people.

Some of our friends might not have a loving family. Or they might have lived through a tragedy we don't know about. They might be struggling with big, uncomfortable feelings. *Be gentle.* Always be kind to each other. And always remind each other to be kind too.

I think my friend is bullying someone!

It can be very hard and confusing when someone we love and enjoy spending time with is being hurtful to someone else.

Here are some things you can do to help:

> **IMMEDIATELY:**
>
> - If your friend is being hurtful to someone with their words, interrupt the conversation. You can tell your friend what they said isn't kind or true. You can also distract your friend by starting to talk about something else.
>
> - If your friend is purposely leaving someone out from games and playdates they arrange, try to include that person in games you arrange. If you feel comfortable, you can also try explaining to your friend that excluding people is not very kind.
>
> - If your friend is physically hurting someone, tell them to stop. If they don't, quickly go get an adult who can help.

LATER:

- Have a think about the kind of relationship you have with your friend. Do you have the kind of friendship where you share opinions and advice with each other? If so, privately discuss with your friend why bullying is bad. Being unkind is a sinful deed that makes Allah unhappy with us. Try to help your friend express themselves kindly. Also try to help them have empathy towards others.

- If you have the kind of friendship where you play together but don't necessarily share opinions and advice with each other, you can ask an elder friend or a grown-up to discuss with everyone in your friend group about why we shouldn't be unkind to each other, and how to help someone if they are being bullied.

- Maybe you can start or join an antibullying group in your school or your community. That way you can help change the kind of thinking that makes kids feel like it's okay to be unkind, or that they can't express themselves without being unkind.

REMEMBER:

- Many times, people don't like it when someone points out their mistakes, so there is a chance your friend may get angry with you at first if you decide to discuss their actions with them. Let your friend have some time to control their emotions. Hopefully, they will understand later what you were trying to say.

- You are only able to control your actions and your boundaries. If your friend keeps on being a bully even after you talk to them, you have to limit the time you spend with them.

Most importantly, remember to always be mindful of Allah. Do good deeds that will make Allah happy with you.

Turn to Allah with your feelings. When you feel happy, say "*Alḥamdulillāh!*" and turn to Allah with *gratitude*. Remind yourself that everything that is good in your life is a blessing and gift from Allah. When you feel sad or afraid or low, say, "*Lā ḥawla wa lā quwwata illā billāh!*" Remind yourself that there is no power or might greater than Allah. No sadness or scary thing is greater than Allah's Love and Mercy. Be mindful of Allah; Allah will protect you.[11]

Select one day of the week. Make sure it is a day when you can take things slow. This is your mindfulness day. Ask your mom, dad, or an elder sibling to help you be mindful on this day.

When you wake up, yawn and shout out "*Alḥamdulillāh!*" You have another chance to be good and do good!

When you get out of bed, say "*Bismillāh!*"

Say "*Bismillāh*" when you start having your meals and your snacks. Say "*Alḥamdulillāh*" when you're done. And say "Thank you" to the person who gave you your food. Give a little kiss and a huge hug if it's a family member!

When you go to play, say "*Alḥamdulillāh!*" What a great blessing it is to have friends. I hope you have an absolute blast!

Take a break to pray. Thank Allah for all these blessings. Ask Allah for even more.

When your day is done, lie down in bed. Think of how your day has been. Have you behaved well the way Allah likes you to behave? Well, *mā shā' Allāh tabāraka Allāh!* How wonderful. May Allah bless you, you amazing person! Say "*Bismillāh*" and close your eyes.

Good night!

BODY BUSINESS

I'm guessing you understand that taking care of yourself also includes taking care of your body.

What are some ways that we do that?

One very important thing that we should do to take care of our bodies is to make sure they get enough energy to work properly. To do that, we have to give them enough water and nutritious food and get plenty of rest.

You see, our body is made up mainly of water. Our brains, our hearts, our skin, even our bones are made up of water. And even though we might not be aware of it, we are always using the water in our body. Water keeps our body cool when the weather is hot or when we are exercising. Water helps digest our food and absorb nutrients. Water helps our blood carry **oxygen** to all our different organs. Water even helps us pee and poo properly.

But if we don't train ourselves to regularly drink water, it can be very easy to forget about rehydrating. Especially if we're busy having fun with friends. That's why I like to set an alarm to remind myself to drink water throughout the day.

Now I like my water completely tasteless and colorless. But maybe you don't. If that's the case, you can put your favorite fruit in a jug of water for about an hour and the water will absorb the fruit's flavor.

Speaking of fruits, what fruits do you like the most? What fruits are easily available to you and your family? Fruits and vegetables contain a lot of important nutrients that help us grow and keep healthy. So remember to have your fruits, veggies, and greens as well.

Also, do remember to have foods that will give you plenty of **carbohydrates** and **proteins**. They give you energy, help you grow, and help your body absorb other nutrients.

Your Healthy Food Pyramid

Creating your own food pyramid is a great way to think of the kinds of food you eat and decide whether they are able to give you the type of nutrition you need.

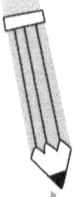

Draw a food pyramid here based on your eating habits.

As a reference, you can use the food pyramids of different cultures provided on www.oldwayspt.org/traditional-diets. There are 5 food pyramids provided on this website that are based on the traditional diets in 5 regions. Find the food pyramid for the region where you are from. What unique diet does your community have? How much does it match the food pyramid on the website? What are the differences?

The traditional diet of any community is usually based on the foods that the community can easily and naturally find where they live. It also provides the energy that the people in that community need to do the kind of work they traditionally do. Do people in your community now do different types of work than they used to do before? Has that changed the diet in your community as well? You may want to get the answers for these questions from someone slightly older... like someone who was around in the 1990s. 😉

> Any health-related information you may read in a book or online is only general information. You may have your own unique requirements. Only a medical professional who knows those requirements can give you specific instructions that you should follow.

I completely understand that there may be some foods you like better than others. There may even be foods you don't like at all. Others may enjoy them, but they are not for you. That's okay, as long as you get all the nutrients you need from the food you do like.

One rule I do follow, though, is to give every type of food at least one go. (As long as it is halal, that is.)

Just as it is important for you to have healthy food and plenty of water, it's also very important that you give your body rest.

Do you sometimes wish there was more time in the day so you could spend more time playing? I think I feel like that most at bedtime, to be honest. You see, when bedtime rolls around, I just wish I could have one more hour to finish reading my new book or enjoying my favorite TV show. But we are only human. We need to give ourselves enough sleep. Otherwise, our bodies will start to feel unwell.

You see, our body and our brain need us to rest. When we sleep, our brain goes to work sorting through the information it collected during the day and storing it all properly. It also replenishes the all-important brain juices that help keep our engines in **shipshape.**

If we haven't had enough restful sleep, we feel groggy and heavy-headed. Even the easiest homework can suddenly feel impossible to do. And you might feel clumsy when playing your favorite sport or practicing your favorite art.

And if we make a habit of not getting good rest, our body will not be able to do the growing it needs to do. Our bodies' defenses (a.k.a. our immune system) will become weaker and it will be easier for germs to attack our body and make us fall sick.

Mission: Restful Sleep

Sleeping comes naturally to most of us. But it always helps to learn ways to improve our natural skills. Here are some tips to level up your sleeping game:

- Try to go to bed around the same time every day—even on weekends. (I know. It's soooo hard.) But our bodies have a built-in clock. By making a habit of sleeping around the same time and waking up around the same time, we're telling our body when to rest and when to wake up. If we sleep late and wake late on the weekends, our clock goes wonky and will not want to be awake in time for school on Monday.

- Turn off your devices at least an hour before bedtime. Our devices are very good at luring us in with exciting games and fun things to do even when our brains need to rest. The blue light that comes from our screens can also delay sleep. It's better to turn off our devices and leave them out of our bedrooms. And to avoid doing other things that could make us feel restless, like reading horror stories right before bedtime.

- Have a calming bedtime routine. Drink a warm glass of milk, read a little, and remember to read your *duʿās* before hitting the sack.

But good food and rest is not all we need! It's equally important that we give our bodies plenty of exercise too.

If you enjoy video games a lot, it's very easy to spend your whole day gaming and not do anything else. But this makes our muscles weaker. It also makes our hearts less healthy and our minds less alert. It can cause us to have less energy, not be able to sleep properly, and develop other serious illnesses as well.

The good news is that exercise isn't just doing push-ups and running laps. It can actually mean playing in the park with your friends. Play catch. Play ball. Go on the monkey bars. Have a swim. All of this is good, fun exercise.

What wonderful blessings Allah has given us! Even having fun is a way for us to take care of ourselves, *alḥamdulillāh*!

Another very important part of taking care of ourselves is keeping ourselves and our surroundings **clean**.

What are some things you do to keep yourself clean? Do you wash your face when you wake up in the morning? Do you brush your teeth twice a day? Do you take showers regularly? Do you wash your hair properly? Do you make sure you wash up properly after you use the toilet? Do you wash your hands with soap after you've been playing outside?

These habits help make sure that we get rid of the **SWEAT**, **DIRT**, and **GERMS** that stick to our bodies as we go about our day. They help keep us fresh. And most importantly, they help keep us healthy.

We also have to make sure that the place we live is clean and tidy. After all, if we live in the middle of rubbish and clutter, it can breed germs that can carry out sneak attacks on us. It can also make us stressed.

As Muslims, we also have to learn an additional type of cleaning up. Cleaning up to prepare for *'ibādah*, or worshiping Allah, in our salah, while reciting Qur'an, or doing things like *ṭawāf* around the Kaaba. To do this type of *'ibadah*, we have to perform *wuḍū'*.

I'm sure you know this already, but let me tell you anyway. We don't necessarily make *wuḍū'* to get rid of dirt or pee or poo from our bodies. Our *wuḍū'* is a reminder that our mistakes might have stained our spirits. It is also a reminder that we have to be as clean as possible in our spirits when we go to perform our *'ibādah*. After all, these *'ibādah* are kind of like we are attending a meeting with Allah. So we try and clean up our spirits by washing the parts of our body that might have made mistakes. Allah ***accepts*** our efforts and forgives our mistakes for us.

When we wash our mouths, Allah forgives us for the mistakes we might have made with our words. He forgives us for looking at things we shouldn't have looked at when we wash our faces, including our eyes. We also wash our ears, with which we might have listened to things we shouldn't have listened to, like someone else's private conversation. When we wash our hands and arms, Allah forgives us for the mistakes we might have made with our hands. For example, you might have let your emotions control your actions and hit your friend, because you were upset with them. Your friend has forgiven you, but you're worried Allah might not have forgiven you. *Alḥamdulillāh*, Allah forgives you as you are doing your *wuḍū'*. And when we wash our feet, Allah forgives us for any mistake we might have used them to walk toward.[12]

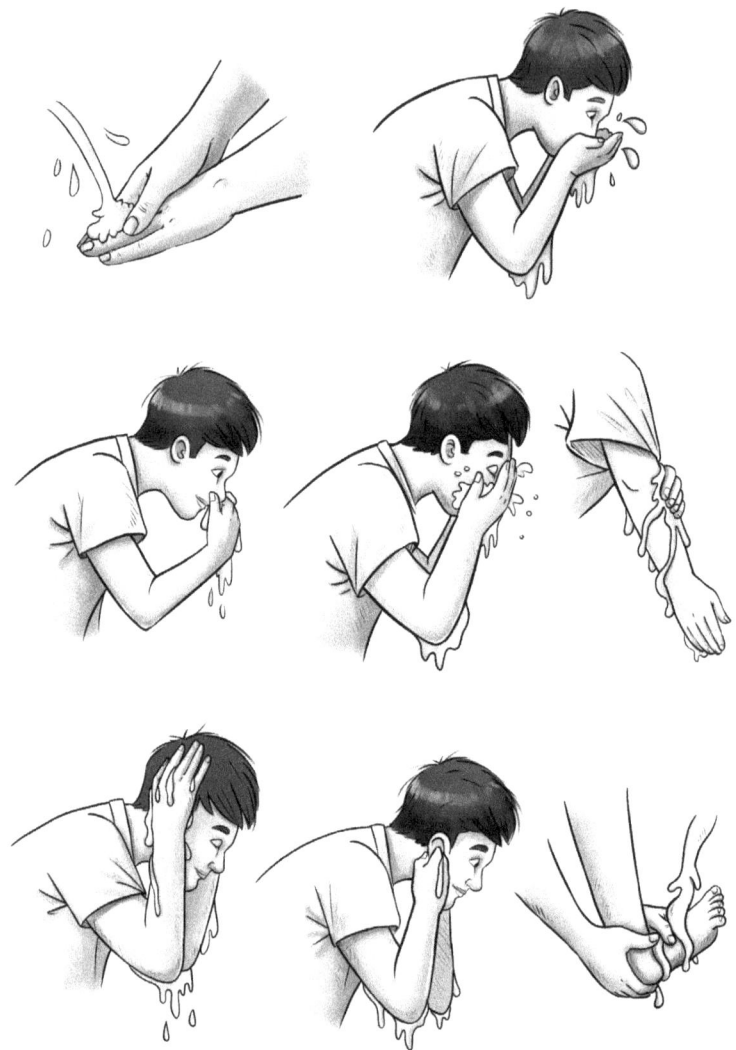

So when you perform your *wuḍū'* from now on, try not to rush through it. Do it slowly and properly. And remember in your heart that you are hoping for Allah to forgive your mistakes because of this *wuḍū'*.

Have you done your *wuḍū'* properly now? *Bārakallāhu fīk*! May Allah bless you, you *beautiful* human being! You are all ready to have a meeting with Allah.

(6)
Everybody Deserves Autonomy

If we were to ever meet each other, would you rather I give you a hug, shake your hand, or give you a high five? Or would you rather we did not do any of those things and just said, "Assalamu alaikum," to each other?

Maybe most grown-ups in your life don't ask you this, or maybe they do. I don't know. But I wanted to ask you this because I think that everybody, even a young person like you, deserves something called **autonomy**.

What is autonomy? I'm glad you asked.

Autonomy is basically a fancy word to say that you get to decide what to do with your own body.

If you remember what we talked about earlier, you will know that Allah *subḥānahu wa taʿālā* blessed us with our bodies. You will also know that Allah made it our responsibility to take care of our bodies, to protect them, and to use them in a way that will please Allah, keep us beneficial to everyone around us, and keep us healthy. We do that by following the rules that Allah sent us through the Prophet *ṣallallāhu ʿalaihi wa sallam*.

Now let's do a little thought experiment. A thought experiment is kind of like a science experiment, but we're going to do it with our imaginations.

Imagine I gave you a treasure chest. Can you picture it? It's full of all kinds of precious gems, pearls, and gold coins. Can you feel how heavy it is? No, no. Don't try to lift it. You might hurt yourself. I don't want you to carry it anywhere. What I want you to do is to take care of it until I come back. Protect it. Only use it to help people do good things. Building a house for a family that needs a home is a good thing. Planting trees is a good thing. Feeding a hungry person is a good thing. But don't do anything bad with it. Like destroying a home. Or buying a chainsaw and cutting down a forest. That, for example, would be a terrible thing to do. So will you protect this treasure chest? You will? That's awesome.

Now imagine there are many other people who want to take that treasure. Some of them want to use it to help people do good things. Other people want to use it for themselves, and not to do good things at all. But here's the catch. You are not allowed to stop people from taking the treasure, even if they don't follow the rules. You're not allowed to say no even if someone wants to take it for themselves. You're not allowed to stop them even if they want to destroy it. But you're still responsible for what happens to the treasure. In fact, I will be very upset with you if it gets destroyed or if it is not used only for good.

Do you think that would be fair?

Of course not. That would be completely **unfair**. *Alḥamdulillāh*, that is what Allah *subḥānahu wa taʿālā* decided about us, our bodies, and ourselves too.

Allah *subḥānahu wa taʿālā* has made everyone responsible for themselves, their bodies, and their actions. In the Qur'an, our actions are described as something we carry. They're kind of like the luggage we carry on our trip to the Hereafter. Every one of us is responsible for our own luggage, which means we get to decide what to pack in our luggage, and what to do with our bodies.

But when we're children, we still have a lot of learning to do about what we should do with our bodies and how. Do you have any baby siblings or cousins? Are they able to decide what to eat, drink, or wear? Do toddlers know when to brush their teeth or take a shower? Do they know not to play with dangerous things or to be careful with easily breakable things like glass? Not at all, right? You were just like that, too, when you were a baby or a toddler.

As we grow older, with the help of grown-ups who love us, we slowly learn to decide and do things by ourselves. And as we learn more about ourselves and the world around us, we get more and more autonomy. We are able to decide and do more and more things on our own.

I'm sure that now you are able to decide and do many things by yourself. *Mā shā' Allāh*! Your parents and everyone who loves you must be so proud of you and so grateful to see you learning to decide and do what is right for you. But there is still a lot of learning to do, and I am sure you're also glad there are grown-ups you can depend on to help you.

But enough about grown-ups for now. I want to tell you about another blessing Allah gave us so that we can decide what is good or bad for our body by ourselves. You know Allah blessed us with five senses, right? We can see with our eyes, hear with our ears, smell with our noses, taste with our tongues, and feel with the nerve endings in our skin. But Allah *subḥānahu wa taʿālā* blessed us with one more sense to help keep us safe. Yes, really. It's our *feelings*. When our feelings are guided and directed by the information we get through the other senses, they become like a sixth sense that can help us keep ourselves safe. *Mā shā' Allāh, alḥamdulillāh.*

So remember, if someone does something to you or tells you to do something that you know or feel isn't safe or right, you are right to firmly say **NO!** That's not rude of you. That's not impolite. And they should absolutely listen to you.

Remember we talked earlier about setting boundaries? When someone hurts your feelings or does things that make you uncomfortable, that person has probably disrespected your natural boundaries. And we already know that you have every right to expect them to respect your boundaries.

If someone ignores your boundaries, even if you didn't specifically ask them not to, please remember that whatever they do is not your fault. It is their fault for not respecting your natural boundaries and taking away your autonomy. It is their fault if their actions hurt you or someone or something.

Please remember also that you don't become bad because of what someone else does. It hurts a lot, that's true. But the hurt you feel is only one part of you. You are so much more than just the hurt.

Also, remember to ask someone for help if you ever are in a situation where your autonomy is taken away. It helps to have a list of grown-ups who you can ask for help if you feel you are in danger. Maybe you can have your parents on that list, or one of them if you want. How about a favorite teacher at school? Or the parent of a friend?

Make a list of grown-ups you trust to help you if you feel you are not safe or your boundaries are not being respected.

You don't have to share this list with anyone. If talking to one grown-up on your list doesn't help, don't give up. Try the next one.

The good news is that a lot of countries now have laws and rules to help protect children's autonomy. So if you ever have someone, even a grown-up, hurting you or taking away your autonomy or privacy, ask one of your most trusted grown-ups to help you. They can help make sure your autonomy and privacy are protected.

(7)
Everybody Needs Healing

Allah *subḥānahu wa taʿālā* created this big, beautiful world for us. The nature around us is beautiful and wondrous. We have amazing bodies and minds to build cozy villages and towns and bustling cities. We are blessed with the love, care, and support of the good people around us. All of these are blessings Allah gave us, so we thank Allah for them by trying our very best to **obey** Him and to **serve** our communities.

At the same time, Allah also created things that can hurt us. For example, in our wonderful environment, there are bacteria and viruses that can make us ill. There may be people in our communities who aren't very kind or caring. Even the people who are loving and caring could accidentally hurt us sometimes. After all, everyone makes mistakes!

So you see, all of us need healing sometimes. Sometimes we need healing because of an illness caused by a virus or bacteria or something to do with our physical body. Other times, we need healing because our feelings have been hurt. We might also need healing for our spirits because of mistakes we have made.

There might also be times when more than one part of us needs healing. After all, our bodies, our minds, and our *spirits* are connected. If one part of us hurts for a very long time, the other parts of us could start hurting too.

We talked earlier about making sure that we don't develop bad habits of doing things that are sinful. But what if we have already developed a **BAD HABIT?** What can we do to break it?

I'd like to tell you how I broke a bad habit, but I feel a little embarrassed. Can you please keep this between us?

I used to have a really bad temper. If someone did something that made me angry, I couldn't control my anger. I would shout. I would throw things. I would basically throw a tantrum. Later, when I calmed down, I would feel really bad about how I behaved. But when I was angry, I felt like an anger monster was controlling me and I couldn't do anything about it.

But I realized that my anger monster was hurting me. It was making me behave badly. It was also hurting the people I love. So I knew I had to control how I reacted to things that made me angry. Feeling angry is okay, but letting my anger be a monster is not.

I decided to learn more about how my anger monster worked. I started paying attention to my anger. I noticed that when I felt angry, I wanted to lash out. This made me feel ashamed. So I would try to ignore my feelings. And while I was ignoring them, my anger would keep growing in the back of my mind until it became the monster I couldn't control.

Instead of letting that happen, I asked my favorite teacher for help, and she taught me how to acknowledge my anger. She also taught me that wanting to lash out was simply a feeling. A feeling isn't something to be ashamed of. It's also not necessarily something I have to act on. Eventually, I learned to sit down and focus on my breathing until I could find better ways to deal with my anger than lashing out.

Bad habits, like throwing **TANTRUMS** when we feel angry, are things that our spirit needs to heal from.

If you think you have more than one habit you want to change, don't try to change everything in one go. That can be very exhausting and overwhelming. Instead, pick one small habit you want to change and focus on that. Once you've changed one small habit, *inshā' Allāh* it'll be easier for you to try to change a bigger one.

Rebooting Our Faith

Sometimes we might develop doubts about our path in life or our faith. This can be very confusing and very painful. But remember, no one's faith is always at the same level. Our level of faith can increase or decrease, but Allah is there for us even in times of confusion or doubt. Remember to ask Allah for guidance in your *duʿās*. Asking adults questions to clear up confusion and doubt and clarify our understanding can help as well.

Our faith increases with good deeds. It also increases with knowledge. So if there are things about Islam that confuse you, try to learn more about them from different, reliable sources. Try not to let your doubts fester. Find a teacher who is gentle and knowledgeable. Explain your doubts to them. Ask them your questions. Keep an open mind. Be sincere in your intention. And always ask Allah for guidance.

Healing Our Minds

We know that when our feelings are hurt, it helps us heal when we share our feelings with loved ones. It also helps us heal when we express our feelings in our writing or art.

But, sometimes, we might not have figured out exactly how we are feeling and don't feel we are able to express our emotions. Or we might be afraid to share our emotions because we are worried about what our loved ones might think of us. Other times, we see everyone around us trying to be strong, so we think it's not acceptable to feel or express our emotions and we may bury them inside.

When this happens, the feelings of hurt or fear we have inside ourselves could multiply the way germs do. They could then make us forget how to feel happy or confident. They could even make us forget how we felt in the good moments in our lives. They might also make us feel AFRAID or NERVOUS all the time. When this happens, it might become an illness in our mind. We call this a mental illness or a mental health condition.

Some of us might not be able to understand the world around us properly. They might see, hear, or feel things that aren't really there, or they may swing from extreme joy or energy to extreme sadness or fatigue. These are also types of mental illnesses or mental health conditions.

Everyone understands physical illnesses very easily. People go to the doctor and perhaps get medicine or other treatments for their physical illnesses and injuries. But for some reason, many people don't acknowledge illnesses that can affect our minds and emotions. This creates **stigma** or shame in our society about mental health conditions. It makes people with mental health conditions feel horrible about themselves. It also makes them afraid to go see a doctor who can help them.

In reality, people who are going through any kind of illness and trying to get better are being very **brave**. So we should always encourage each other to get the help we need.

Remember, Allah *subḥānahu wa taʿālā* created this world and made us part of it. And it is part of Allah's wisdom that illnesses and their treatments also exist in our world. So it's just silly to make each other feel bad about falling ill.

Also remember, it is with Allah's will and power that all medicines and treatments work. We should take the medication and follow the treatment plans our doctors give us, but we should always ask Allah to help us feel better. He is *al-Shāfī*, the Healer, and our complete trust should be in Him.

Growing Pains

(8)
Everybody Grows Up

Do your parents, grandparents, and aunties and uncles ever tell you how amazed they are at how grown up you've become? "Look at you!" they may say when you meet them after a long time. Or they may even tell you how small you were when you were born and wonder at how big and tall you are now.

Well, that's all part of growing up, *alḥamdulillāh*. And everyone is always in the process of becoming older and growing up.

I'm sure you know that as we grow up, our body is changing in many ways. For example, did you know that a baby's body will have almost 100 more bones than a grown-up's body does? You see, when we are born, our bodies have about 300 separate bones that are held together by something a bit softer called "cartilage." As we grow older, there are some parts of the body where those separate bones will fuse and become one bone. In the end, most grown-ups wind up having 206 bones altogether.

Another change that happens in our body as we grow older is in hormone levels. Hormones are chemicals that our bodies produce and need. Each hormone carries different messages around the body, telling different body parts to do different things.

For example, there is a hormone called **insulin** that is produced in an organ we call the pancreas. It helps transport glucose from our blood to our cells, where it can be transformed into energy. Insulin makes sure that just the right amount of glucose goes in our cells and packs the rest of it away in our liver to be used later. If our body doesn't have enough insulin or isn't able to use insulin properly, our cells won't be able to take glucose from our blood and our blood sugar level will become too high. Then our bodies won't be able to pack away the extra glucose and that creates a condition called "diabetes." One of the treatments for diabetes is to give insulin injections.

Other types of hormones are related to growing up. These hormones tell our bodies to begin the process we know of as "puberty." **Puberty** begins around the time we are tweens and continues into our teenage years. It is basically a growth spurt where our bodies grow in many different ways. It shows that we aren't children anymore and that we should start getting ready to be adults.

When we reach a certain age, a little pea-sized gland in our brain releases hormones that tell our body that we are now ready (or almost ready) to be grown-ups.

Remember we talked earlier about our reproductive systems? During puberty we will notice a lot of changes in our bodies that are connected to our reproductive systems.

You see, when puberty starts, the hormones our brain releases travel through our bloodstream all the way to the reproductive system. When the male reproductive system receives the hormonal signal from the brain, the testicles will start producing sperm and a lot of a hormone called **testosterone**. When the female reproductive system receives the hormonal signal from the brain, the ovaries will start producing a lot of the hormone called *estrogen* and releasing one ovum (egg) almost every month. These are all signals that you are now about to be able to take on more responsibilities.

Slowly, our bodies will begin to experience changes.

We will start to grow hair in all sorts of "odd" places, which are actually not odd at all. You probably don't have hair under your arms or in the area around your genitals now, but you can expect some to start growing there when puberty begins. And that hair will become thicker and coarser as time goes on. That is normal in all bodies, male and female.

In Islam, we are advised to remove this hair in a safe and hygienic way. Once again, remember: It is not because having this hair is shameful or ugly. It is simply that the Prophet Muḥammad ṣallallāhu ʿalaihi wa sallam advised us to remove it as part of our **hygiene**. He said it is part of our *fiṭrah* to remove the hair growing in our armpits and our pubic area.[13] *Fiṭrah* is the word for the natural inclinations of our minds and souls.

> **What do I do about my hairy legs?**
>
> Most of us have some amount of hair on our bodies. This hair can be very fine and barely visible, or it can be thick and coarse. Most of the time, it just depends on our genetics.
>
> Sometimes body hair or a lack of it can be an indication of a hormone imbalance. So if you are worried that your body hair isn't normal, it's good to ask your doctor about it.
>
> Remember that having body hair is not something to be ashamed of. It is perfectly natural. You don't have to remove it if you don't want to. But feel free to remove it if you feel more comfortable that way.

There are many ways to remove your armpit and pubic hair (or any body hair that you feel you need to remove).

The easiest and most common way of removing unwanted body hair is shaving. Of course, it helps if you have someone with some shaving experience to show you how it's done. But, just in case, **let me give you a few shaving tips that have been passed down through the generations:**

> Always prepare the skin before you start shaving. Wet your skin and apply a shaving gel or lotion before you begin. Shaving with dry skin can easily cause nicks or skin irritation.
>
> Use slow, short, gentle strokes of your razor *against* the direction of the hair growth to get a close shave. Never stroke the razor blade sideways on your skin. That can cut you. Remember to rinse your blade between strokes to make shaving easier and more hygienic.
>
> Once you're done shaving, pat your skin dry with a soft, clean towel. You can use an aftershave lotion if you want. But be aware that using fragrance on your skin right after shaving can sting, due to tiny nicks the razor may make.
>
> Clean your razor, pat it dry, and store it properly. Disposable razors and blades should be thrown away after three or more uses.
>
> Remember: We can share many things with our friends and family. But not used razors. That's just gross! They can carry germs and bacteria from one person to the other and cause skin problems and infections.

You might also notice that you are now starting to get whiteheads and blackheads. These happen because of a skin condition called **ACNE**. Acne can occur during times of hormonal change in our body, like the start of puberty.

Our skin has millions of tiny little wells called "pores." These pores connect the surface of our skin to oil glands that lay under our skin. The oil glands produce oil and help move dead skin cells to the surface of our skin so we can wash them away and keep our skin nice and clean.

Sometimes, these glands can produce too much oil. Our pores can then get clogged with the oil and some dead skin cells. When the clogged pore is exposed to air, it dries and becomes a blackhead. If the pore collects bacteria, which then multiplies and causes a little infection, it is called a whitehead. These are awkward but fairly normal and treatable.

Taking good care of your skin by keeping it clean and moisturized can usually (but not always!) help keep acne under control.

Going to the drugstore to buy a cleanser or moisturizer for your skin can be daunting, especially the first time. There are so many brands, and they make all sorts of claims just to sell their products. But normally you don't need expensive skincare products to take good care of your skin. An affordable cleanser that doesn't leave your skin feeling stripped and tightened and a moisturizer that rehydrates your skin are just what you need. This is prime elder sibling, aunt or uncle, or slightly older friend territory. Ask them for help figuring out skin care on your next trip to the drugstore.

Taking care of your skin also includes being careful about the food you eat. Increase fruits, vegetables, and greens in your diet. Try to limit oils, sodas, and food that have added **sugar**.

Of course none of this means your acne will be 100% controlled. Acne can be genetic. If you have a lot of acne and it affects your self-confidence, you can get help from a doctor to treat it. But remember, your worth as a person is based on your character. You are a beautiful person as long as your character is beautiful.

As a Boy Becomes a Man

In the male body, facial hair also starts to become thicker and darker, eventually becoming a beard. The voice box in our throat also becomes a little larger in the male body. This is why you will notice many men have an "Adam's apple" that is larger and more prominent than most women's.

Changes happen in the genitals as well. The testicles will grow slightly bigger than they were before. The penis will also become a little longer and wider. These are normal changes and nothing to worry about at all.

Another slightly awkward change might be having erections and what is called "wet dreams."

An erection simply means that more blood goes to the veins in your penis. Because your body is adjusting to being a grown-up's body, you might get erections randomly. This can be very awkward in public. The good news is that it will go away by itself in a little while.

Wear properly-fitted underwear and loose trousers when you go out. This helps keep your private parts private. You can also adjust your shirt, bag, or books to cover yourself up. Some people say that it helps to distract yourself with other thoughts instead of worrying about the erection. But if you are uncomfortable, there's nothing wrong with simply **excusing** yourself and going to the restroom.

Sometimes your body releases semen while you're asleep. You might find a small wet spot on the bed when you wake up. This is called a nocturnal emission or a "wet dream." It's not the same as peeing yourself. It's just another way your body is trying to adjust to being a grown-up's body.

Having a wet dream does mean that you will need to take a shower or bath and make *ghusl* before you pray or read Qur'an. You can always ask your parents or another older person to teach you more about performing *ghusl* after a wet dream. You don't want to miss any prayer time and you want to always be able to read Qur'an, so it's important that you make your *ghusl* as soon as you can.

 **The How-Tos of *Ghusl***

1. Have the intention in your heart to perform *ghusl* so you can pray, read Qur'an, etc. Although you're just taking a shower, this shower is special because you're doing it in obedience to Allah *subḥānahu wa taʿālā*. Say *bismillāh* (or, if your shower is joined together with a toilet, think it).

2. Wash your hands first. If you touched any of the seminal fluid on your body, on the bed, or on your clothes, wash it away.

3. Wash your private area and remove any wet spots or dried up fluids you have on that area or any part of your body.

4. Perform *wuḍū'* the way you would to prepare for prayer.

5. Pour water on your head. Run your fingers through your hair and make sure that your scalp is completely wet.

6. Now, pour water on the rest of your body, starting with the right side. Scrub your body gently with your hands or a loofah or washcloth and make sure every part of your body is wet.

You can then use soap and shampoo if you want. But for *ghusl*, the most important thing is to make sure you wash your whole body with water.

7. You can wash your feet separately when you step out of the shower if the water puddled up at your feet.

Remember to be mindful of your water consumption. Water is an important resource Allah *subḥānahu wa taʿālā* blessed us with. Don't waste it, even if you have unlimited access to it. Remember, there are many people around the world, sometimes even in our own communities, who are struggling to access clean water. The Prophet *ṣallallāhu ʿalaihi wa sallam* used to make his *ghusl* with less than 3 liters of water!

How much water do you think you use during a 10-minute shower? How much water would a bath require? (Look these up on the internet—the answers may surprise you!) Would a shower or bath be better and closer to the Prophet's practice of conserving water during *ghusl*?

You might wake up in the middle of the night and find that you've had a wet dream. You can wash the areas where the fluid touched, make *wuḍū'*, and go back to bed if you'd prefer. You can then perform your *ghusl* right before praying your Fajr. Sleep is important for a growing body like yours. Don't disrupt your sleep any more than necessary.

Now that you are older, you have to pay even more attention to praying your salah on time and completing your fasts. You have completed the practice time you had when you were younger and are now completely **RESPONSIBLE** to Allah for your *'ibādah*.

Learning to Walk in a Woman's Body

In the female body, when puberty starts, the uterus starts to develop extra tissue inside it. (No, not Kleenex, silly. What I mean by tissue is a collection of similar cells.) This is the same kind of tissue a baby would use to get its energy from its mother's food while it is developing inside the mother's tummy. One of the ovaries will then release an egg cell. Because there are no sperm inside the body, the egg cell will not develop into a baby. So the womb will let go of the egg cell and the extra tissue it has prepared just in case there was a baby.

This tissue will come out of the vagina along with some blood. This is called "menstruation." An easier name for this process is your "period." Getting your period will look like you're bleeding into your underwear. It can be very scary if you don't know what it is. But, *alḥamdulillāh*, you know what it is now. You know that it's something completely normal and natural. You also know that it's actually only very little blood and mostly extra tissue that your body doesn't need.

Simply ask your parents or a grown-up you trust for pads to keep your private parts clean during this time so your clothes won't get stained. They will help you. That is the beautiful thing about parents and grown-ups who love you. They are there to help you get through the difficult and **awkward** parts of life.

There are many different types of menstrual products these days. Some of them are disposable. You use them once and throw them away. They include disposable pads and tampons. Others are reusable. They include menstrual underwear, reusable pads, and menstrual cups. Some of these products may be easier for young women to use than others.

Discuss with a grown-up and decide which product (or products) are most suitable for you and find out how to use them properly.

What would you have done if you had gotten your period blood on the Prophet's luggage?!

Once, Prophet Muḥammad ṣallallāhu ʿalaihi wa sallam was traveling with some of his companions. It was a long trip, so people were sharing camels. The Prophet ṣallallāhu ʿalaihi wa sallam offered to let a girl, who was maybe about your age, ride on his camel with him. She sat on top of his bags.

When they stopped for some rest and the girl got down from the camel, she realized she had gotten her first ever period while they were on the road. To her horror, there was blood on the Prophet's luggage!! She was so embarrassed that she tried to hide behind the camel.

The Prophet ṣallallāhu ʿalaihi wa sallam noticed that she was hiding. He asked her, "What happened?" She was too ashamed to reply. So he looked around to check what was going on and noticed the blood on his bag. "Did you just get your period?"

She meekly replied, "Yes."

The Prophet ṣallallāhu ʿalaihi wa sallam didn't get upset with her. He gently told her to ask a woman for some menstrual protection she could use. Then he advised her to just wash the stain on his luggage with water and salt—back then, they didn't use to have detergent like we do now— and come take her seat on his luggage for the rest of the way.

By doing this, the Prophet ṣallallāhu ʿalaihi wa sallam taught her that staining your clothes or your seat during periods is not something to be ashamed of. It could happen to anyone, after all. He also showed her how to clean up a leak if it does happen. The Prophet ṣallallāhu ʿalaihi wa sallam was such a kind and gentle teacher, mā shā' Allāh![14]

> **Preparing Your First Period Kit**
>
> There's no specific age when girls get their first period. It's understandable that you may worry about not being ready when it happens. You can ease your mind a bit if you prepare a little, though.
>
> - Before you get your period, learn how to use a pad. Ask a grown-up to show you how or follow the instructions on the package.
>
> - Keep a pad and a small hand towel or napkin handy for when your period arrives each month. Keep a candy or some ice-cream money, too, if you'd like. Your body is doing something hard and special. Ice cream or chips will be a well-deserved celebratory treat.

Menstruation is something that happens in the female body approximately every month or so. That's why periods are sometimes called **monthly periods**. You will notice that your periods last for a few days every time—usually around three to seven days. This is normal too.

The duration from the beginning of one period to the beginning of the next is your monthly cycle. When girls begin menstruating, their bodies may need a little bit of time for their cycles to become regular. For a while they might even have irregular periods that come any old time rather than sticking to a monthly schedule. Tracking your periods—what day they begin and how long they last—is a great way to learn your body's **rhythm** and predict when the next period should arrive.

Keep a small calendar or a period tracking app on your phone. When you get your period, put an X or any cool mark that you want on the first date of your period. Mark every additional day that you have bleeding as well. Repeat this the following month. Now count from the first day of your period in the first month to the first day of your period in the second month. This is the length of your cycle. Most women tend to have a monthly cycle of around 28 days. But it can range anywhere between 21 days and 40 days.

Although some girls may naturally have irregular periods, there are some health conditions that can cause them as well. So if you experience irregular periods for three or more months in a row, it's best to visit the doctor and have a checkup.

The level of hormones related to a girl's menstrual cycle change every day throughout the month. That's why, as you get closer to having your periods, you may feel a little uncomfortable. You may feel slightly more tired. You may feel a bit more emotional—sometimes even moody. You may feel bloated and gassy in your stomach. You may even have stomach cramps. You may even notice that you have acne breakouts during particular times of your cycle. These are things that can be uncomfortable. But, normally, with the love and care of your family and people around you, you will be able to manage them. If you are not able to, let your family know so they can take you to a doctor, who can help you with them.

All in all, try to be gentle with yourself. Allah *subḥānahu wa taʿālā* is *al-Hakīm*, the Most Wise. That is why Allah is also gentle with us during our periods. When we are having periods, we don't have to pray our five daily salah. And we don't have to make them up later, either. We also don't have to fast during Ramadan on the days when we are having periods. But we do make up for those missed fasts after Ramadan.

After you finish your period, you should make *ghusl* and return to praying. Don't forget to make up any missed Ramadan fasts, as well. Girls make *ghusl* after finishing our periods the same way boys do *ghusl* after having a wet dream. And just like having wet dreams is perfectly normal and nothing to be embarrassed about, having your period is perfectly normal as well. This is the way Allah created us. We just need to know how to take care of ourselves, as our bodies work the way Allah intended for them to work.

And just because you aren't praying or fasting during your periods, it does not mean that you have to feel disconnected from Allah either. No matter what you're going through, you can always remember Allah in your heart. You can also talk to Allah in *duʿā* and say your *adhkār*. These forms of *prayer* are always open for us no matter what.

> Some *adhkār*: *Subḥānallāh. Alḥamdulillāh. Lā ilāha illa Allāh. Allāhu akbar. Astaghfirullāh.*

Once your first period is over, you should start paying extra attention to offering all your prayers on time and being responsible for your *'ibādah*.

Another change that happens in the female body that is related to reproduction is breast development. During childhood, both male and female bodies have flat chests. When puberty starts, the **hormones** that a girl's body produces send a signal for her breasts to begin developing into more adult female breasts. This is because if a woman becomes a mother, she will often need to breastfeed her baby. When your breasts start developing, they can feel a little sore. It can hurt if someone bumps your chest or accidentally runs into you. This is normal and these "growing pains" usually go away as you get older.

If you are worried about any of your body's changes, remember that it is okay to talk to your **elders** and share your feelings. It's also okay to ask to see a doctor. The doctor can do a checkup to make sure your body is developing well. The doctor can also recommend the kinds of food you can eat and activities you can do to make the process of growing easier for your body.

You remember how we said earlier that puberty is a growth spurt, right? That means you may gain some weight during puberty. This isn't an unhealthy weight gain, so don't try to lose that weight by dieting or overexercising. That can actually end up being unhealthy.

Something else you should keep in mind is that different people grow at different speeds. Your puberty may start slightly earlier or slightly later than your friends'. That's okay. You also know that different people have different shapes and sizes of bodies. So the amount of growing different people do during puberty is also bound to be different. That's okay too.

Outgrowing the Nest

While our body is going through puberty, our mind also does a lot of growing up. Your mind will also realize that you're not a child anymore—which means that you will probably want more space for yourself. You will have more thoughts you don't necessarily want to share with your parents. There is nothing wrong with that. But I hope you do try to understand something: just like you are learning to grow up, your parents are learning how to help you grow up. And it can be challenging for them too.

Your parents worry for you. So always let them know that you will reach out to them if you're ever in trouble or needing help.

It might be hard to talk face-to-face with your parents about certain things. If that's the case, you can write them a letter or send them a text. The important thing is that you **communicate** with them, especially when you need help.

You might also start to question your parents' **views** about things. This is also a natural part of learning to be your own person. As long as you remember to be respectful, there is no harm in having or expressing different opinions. As you keep growing older, you might find that you understand your parents' perspective better. You might even end up agreeing with them a lot more than you thought you ever would.

Speaking of hard things to talk to your parents about, you will probably start thinking about sex during puberty. Your thoughts aren't wrong or dirty. Sex is the natural biological process for human reproduction to happen. We know Allah created us to be able to **reproduce**, so that means Allah created us to have these thoughts about sex starting from puberty. Once again, like every other awkward thing about puberty, these feelings are also completely normal and natural.

Although sex is biologically needed for reproduction, it isn't *only* for reproduction. In Islam, adults are allowed to have sex when they are married to each other, and they can do it just because it feels good to express their mutual love for each other in that way.

Of course you will be curious about the details of sex. You will keep learning about those details as you grow older. Just remember to get the details from trusted people who will give you the correct information. Sometimes you may hear things from friends or from the internet that aren't completely true. So always **double-check** with an adult you can trust when you hear things from friends or read them online.

It isn't bad to ask questions or look for information on this topic. In fact, the Messenger of Allah ṣallallāhu 'alaihi wa sallam was always willing to have respectful, honest, and open discussions about puberty, reproduction, and sex with his companions. He didn't get upset with them for having questions.[15] There are even verses in the Qur'an that talk about these topics.[16]

> The Prophet's companions followed his example of talking frankly about sexual topics when they were teaching those who came after them, and we should follow that example today, as well.

Actions Speak Louder than Thoughts

Allah has instructed us to not let the thoughts we have about sex and our sexual attractions control our behavior. We can't decide what thoughts we have or what our desires are, so *alḥamdulillāh*, we are not judged based on them. But we can **control** how we act, and we will be judged based on that.

You will notice that there's a lot of preoccupation with sex in our society. In film, art, music, and even billboards and shop fronts, people seem to try to make everything look "sexy." This naturally makes it harder for us to control our desires. It can also affect how we perceive ourselves and make us think negatively about our own bodies.

I hope you will always remember what we said earlier about your body. It is a gift from Allah, and it is a part of Allah's wonderful and beautiful creation. The pictures and videos you see on TV, social media, or magazine covers are posed and edited with apps and specialized software. They don't show the reality of human bodies. And besides, our job in this world isn't to look good or judge whether other people look good. It is to *do* good for Allah's sake. And hopefully we can all feel beautiful and grateful while doing it.

> *Alḥamdulillāh*, Allah has already blessed us with beautiful bodies. Let's ask Him to bless us with beautiful characters as well.

Remember: In Islam, we are all instructed to lower our gaze. This means that we shouldn't look at other people's *'awrah,* even if they are not covering it. We simply look away.[17]

But of course that doesn't mean that we are *never* allowed to have romantic or sexual relationships. As we discussed earlier, Allah has given us a way to respectfully have an intimate romantic and sexual relationship with someone of the opposite sex. He has created a way for us to do so responsibly and in a way that protects everyone's rights. That is **marriage**.

But marriage is not only meant to be a way to have a sexual relationship with someone. It is also a huge responsibility. When you get married, you have responsibilities toward your spouse and your spouse has responsibilities toward you. And if you have children together, you both have responsibilities as parents. So you both need to be physically and emotionally **mature** so that you can fulfill your family's rights and live up to the responsibilities that come with marriage and parenthood. All in due time, of course.

You may have crushes and imagine that you would be very happy if you got married to this boy or that girl. But those feelings are fluttering feelings most of the time. Teenage crushes are often a result of your brain and your emotions trying to be a grown-up. They are dreams, but we don't have to make them a reality. We can choose to not act on them just yet. You have so much to do and achieve for yourself before you have to take on the responsibilities that come with the kind of intimate relationship that is part of marriage.

In the meantime, you can fill your time with *'ibādah* and learn more about yourself, your unique talents and abilities, and your needs. Build yourself up with knowledge and experience. Spend time with your friends. Volunteer. Be a source of **goodness** and an agent of **service** in your community.

When You're Almost Grown...

When we start puberty, we also get to start following the rules of privacy and covering our ʿawrah a bit more seriously.

If you're a boy, you will notice that Muslim women who are not from your immediate family will now begin to cover their hair, arms, and legs in front of you. You might have been allowed to sit with your mom's friends before, for example, even when they were not fully covered. But once you start puberty, you will need to give them more space, so they can cover themselves up properly in front of you. Doing this is part of respecting their boundaries.

If you're a girl, you will be on the opposite end of the boys' experience. You will begin covering most of your body in front of men who are not members of your immediate family.[18] Allah has asked us to do this so we will be **recognized** as women of faith, whose attention is on their primary purpose in this life: to worship Allah subḥānahu wa taʿālā.

> Whether you are a boy or a girl, it's also important that you don't spend time alone with someone from the other sex who is not from your immediate family. This is not meant to be disrespectful to others. We do this because we consider protecting our spiritual self from sin to be one of our most important responsibilities. We also accept that shayṭān is always trying to convince us to make mistakes. He might use our desire for romantic or sexual closeness to make us slip up. After all, wanting romantic and sexual closeness is something that is naturally part of us.[19] And controlling those desires is much easier when we don't open the door for shayṭān by being alone with someone from the other sex.

Sometimes it can be hard to follow the Islamic rules of dressing. It can also be hard to respect the boundaries for interaction between boys and girls, especially in our modern environment. People around us will tell us these rules aren't important. They may say there are just too many rules and they're too tough, or even that they're unhealthy.

For me, it helps to remember that Allah accepts all our efforts to follow the rules of Islam and multiplies the rewards for us. And that establishing yourself as a person of faith from the very beginning, by the way you dress, helps ward off awkward situations later, like having to explain why you don't want to go out and do haram things with your friends. I also try to remember that Islam doesn't demand that we have absolutely no interaction with people of the opposite sex. We are simply asked to keep our interactions naturally respectful and professional in a way that doesn't potentially lead us into *shayṭān's* trap.

Alḥamdulillāh, we are blessed with many Muslim men and women who are knowledgeable in Islam and can teach us. Many of them even have public discussions to talk about some of the things we deal with as we are growing up. Many of them also give classes online. Find the Islamic scholars in your own community and learn from them.

> Rabata, Safina Society, and Suhaib Webb Institute of Sacred Sciences (SWISS) offer English-language lessons on Islamic topics for young people online. Al-Salam Institute, DeepDeen.tv, Jannah Institute, Suhbah Institute, Yaqeen Institute for Islamic Research, Seeker's Guidance, and others also have informative articles, videos, and lectures on Islamic topics by knowledgeable scholars. These are only some of the reliable Islamic resources available online. Ask for help finding good Islamic resources from adults around you who are knowledgeable in Islam.

Many of our communities put a lot of focus on girls' modesty. But boys should remember that they must be modest as well and keep their focus on living their lives for Allah's sake. Islamically, boys are no more allowed to enhance their bodies and show off than girls are.

In the meantime, remember that everyone your age is going through a slightly confusing and difficult time in their life. Someone might come to school with an angry red pimple on their face. Someone else could get their period in the middle of class and stain their clothes. Someone might feel tall and lanky and all kinds of awkward in their body. Someone might be worried they aren't growing at the same speed as everyone else. Someone else might be feeling moody, because growing up is so incredibly confusing and hard.

Be easygoing with yourself. Be gentle with your friends. Be kind to your classmates. If you have a compliment to offer, be sure to offer it. If you have a suggestion or **constructive criticism**, give it kindly and privately.

If we are kind to each other, we can make all this a little easier for everyone.

How Can I Be a Good Muslim Online?

As we grow older, we have more and more access to online platforms where we can express ourselves and connect with other people. When we're online, we have to take care of ourselves and be mindful of our actions, just like we do when we're offline.

Remember to maintain the privacy and security settings on all your online accounts.

Be mindful of what you share, what you access, and how you interact with people online. Sometimes it can feel easier to write hurtful things about people than to say hurtful things to them. But remember. The people you're interacting with online are not "bots." They are real people like you and me.

And most importantly, Allah is *al-Khabīr*, the Most Well-Aware of everything, including our behavior online. Allah promises comfort for our spirits and Jannah for our souls in the Hereafter. Try to be worthy and deserving of Allah's reward. Be a positive force in the virtual space, just like you are a force for good in real life.

And lastly, remember to disconnect. There's a whole world outside of our screens that is waiting for us. Don't become so engrossed in your online presence that you forget to live outside of it. Give your eyes a break. Give your brain some rest. Give your body a shake. You deserve it.

(9)
Everybody Has a Role to Play

I wonder. Would you say you're more of a shy and reserved person? Or do you think you're more of a boisterous and feisty firecracker? Do you enjoy tinkering with gadgets and fixing things up around the house, or would you prefer spending your holiday baking tasty goodies for your family or friends?

Don't worry. No answer you give is going to be a wrong answer. It's just a matter of doing what you enjoy. Allah *subḥānahu wa taʿālā* created all of us with different **personalities** and interests. Those personality traits and interests are not necessarily gendered. One boy may be boisterous and loud, while another boy may be shy and gentle. One girl may enjoy cooking elaborate meals, while another may prefer spending her day in a garage helping to fix up an old car. The important thing is to rely on your personality and interests to be your strengths.

You will notice that many people think there is a certain way to be a man or a woman.

For example, some people think that boys shouldn't cry, feel fear, or ask for help; they think that only girls should be seen expressing their emotions or have moments of "weakness." Have you ever heard the phrase "**Man up!**" being used to tell a boy or man to be strong? "Boys don't cry," they say. Some of these people also think that boys can't be shy or reserved. They think that all boys have to be boisterous and loud, and that all boys who don't fit that mold are a little "girly."

These people often think that girls also have to be a certain way in order to be "proper" girls. For example, they expect all girls to be shy. They think that girls shouldn't have strong opinions and that they shouldn't try to explain their point of view. If a girl does that, they might say that she is "bossy" or "argumentative." They also might say that all girls are weak. That's why, for example, they think that being *like a girl* is a bad thing for a boy.

These ideas are only some examples of what is known as "gender stereotypes." They are **oversimplified** ideas about what it means to be a boy or man, or a girl or woman. What other examples of gender stereotypes have you seen or heard in your community?

It's important for us to remember that many gender stereotypes are based only on culture. They do not represent Islamic teachings. In fact, sometimes they might even be contrary to Islamic teachings about gender.

Things like this can be confusing and hard to figure out. How can we tell the difference between what our culture tells us and what Islam teaches us? How can we be sure we are actually following Allah's commands and not just our family or community's traditional beliefs?

To figure this out, we have to look in the Qur'an and the teachings of the Prophet Muḥammad ṣallallāhu 'alaihi wa sallam. We also have to look at the practice of his companions raḍiyallāhu 'anhum and the practice of the early scholars, who were students of the companions. Of course we can ask people who are experts in Islamic studies, but it's still good to know what they study to figure these things out, right? After all, we should be thinkers, not blind followers.

Let's look at examples of important people who have been mentioned in the Qur'an. Allah subḥānahu wa ta'ālā gives us examples of both good people and bad people, and these people were men as well as women. **Being good or bad doesn't depend on being a man or a woman.**

Among the examples of bad people Allah gives us in the Qur'an are even family members of prophets and messengers 'alaihimussalām (may peace be upon them). For example, one of the sons of Nūḥ 'alaihissalām refused to believe in Allah and follow His commands. And even though his father was a prophet, he was punished for his actions.[20]

Another example of disbelieving people in the Qur'an is the wife of Lūṭ 'alaihissalām. She also refused to believe in Allah and follow His commands. And she was punished as well.[21]

On the other hand, when Allah sets an example of someone who *did* believe sincerely and follow Allah's command, He tells us of the wife of a notorious disbeliever and tyrant—the Pharaoh during the time of Musa *'alaihissalām*. Although her husband disbelieved in Allah and committed all kinds of injustices as a leader, she chose to believe in Allah. Then she made *du'ā* and asked Allah, "My Lord, build a home in Jannah for me that is close to You." She knew that no matter how badly her husband behaved, she could decide for herself what she would believe in and how she would act. She chose to be a believer, and Allah both **comforted** and **rewarded** her.[22]

This goes to show that no matter who our family members are or how they behave, we are judged only on our own actions. And that is how we will be judged for fulfilling our role in this life. On our actions.

When we look at the life of the Prophet Muḥammad *ṣallallāhu 'alaihi wa sallam* and the lives of his companions *raḍiyallāhu 'anhum*, we can see that they didn't follow many of the gender stereotypes that we have in our communities.

Have you heard about 'Uthmān ibn 'Affān *raḍiyallāhu 'anhu*? He was one of the first people to become Muslim. He was the son-in-law of the Messenger of Allah, which means he married the Prophet's daughter.

Did you know that 'Uthmān was a very shy man? One day, the Messenger of Allah *ṣallallāhu 'alaihi wa sallam* was lying down resting in his home. Of course we all understand that when we lie down and are relaxing, sometimes our clothes will rise up and part of our legs might show. That's not a problem, right?

Well, the Prophet's clothes were slightly lifted, too, and part of his legs were showing. While the Prophet *ṣallallāhu 'alaihi wa sallam* was resting like this, Abū Bakr *raḍiyallāhu 'anhu* came for a visit and asked if he could come in. The Prophet *ṣallallāhu 'alaihi wa sallam* stayed lying down and allowed him in. After a while, 'Umar *raḍiyallāhu 'anhu* came to visit as well. The Prophet *ṣallallāhu 'alaihi wa sallam* allowed him in without getting up as well. Of course, as all polite visitors do, they didn't stay too long. After a while, they left.

A little while later, 'Uthmān *raḍiyallāhu 'anhu* came visiting and said *salām*. The Prophet *ṣallallāhu 'alaihi wa sallam* sat up and straightened his clothes before he let 'Uthmān in. The Prophet's wife, 'Ā'ishah *raḍiyallāhu 'anhā* noticed this. So when 'Ūthmān left, she asked the Prophet *ṣallallāhu 'alaihi wa sallam* why he didn't sit up and straighten his clothes when Abū Bakr and 'Umar came, but did when 'Uthmān came. The Prophet *ṣallallāhu 'alaihi wa sallam* explained to her that "'Uthmān is a shy man." The Prophet *ṣallallāhu 'alaihi wa sallam* was afraid that if he were lying down, 'Uthmān might feel awkward about disturbing him and leave right away, without discussing whatever he had come to discuss.[23] He didn't tell him that he shouldn't be shy just because he's a man. He didn't tell him to "Man up!" Instead, because he knew he was shy, he made considerations for him and avoided making him feel awkward.

Not only that. Being a shy person didn't prevent 'Uthmān from being a brave warrior or a strong leader. 'Uthmān *raḍiyallāhu 'anhu* was the third **CALIPH** (leader) of the Muslims after the Messenger of Allah *ṣallallāhu 'alaihi wa sallam* passed away.

When we read about the life of the Prophet *ṣallallāhu 'alaihi wa sallam*, we also learn that housework is the responsibility of men just as it is women. In fact, the Messenger of Allah *ṣallallāhu 'alaihi wa sallam* himself did housework. He sewed and patched his clothes and fixed his slippers when they needed mending. He used to milk the goat and bring the milk to his family. When his wife was asked how he behaved at home, she simply said that he served his family like any other person would. For her, his behavior was simply good behavior. He wasn't being "manly" or "womanly." He was simply being a responsible member of the family. Then, of course, when it was time for prayer, he went to the mosque to offer his salah.[24]

So regardless of our gender, as members of Muslim families, we must learn and do the chores in our homes. That is part of the role we have to play as responsible people who can take care of themselves, their surroundings, and their loved ones.

The Prophet *ṣallallāhu 'alaihi wa sallam* showed that being openly caring and affectionate is also something that isn't gender-specific. He used to openly say that he loved his family and friends. One day, someone asked him who he loved the most. Without a second thought, he replied, "My wife, 'Ā'ishah." The person asked him who he loved most among his friends. He replied, "I love Abū Bakr." The person asked him who next, and he replied, "'Umar."[25]

The Prophet ṣallallāhu 'alaihi wa sallam would also openly express his love for his children and grandchildren. Many people in his society had the idea that men should be tough and not show affection to their families—especially in public. Prophet Muḥammad ṣallallāhu 'alaihi wa sallam taught them better.

One day, a man called al-Aqra' raḍiyallāhu'anhu came to the Messenger of Allah ṣallallāhu 'alaihi wa sallam and sat with him. The Messenger ṣallallāhu 'alaihi wa sallam had his grandson, al-Hasan ibn 'Ali raḍiyallāhu'anhumā, on his lap. He cuddled and kissed him.

Al-Aqra' was slightly shocked. He told Prophet Muḥammad ṣallallāhu 'alaihi wa sallam that he had ten children and had never kissed any of them, even once.

The Prophet ṣallallāhu 'alaihi wa sallam knew what he meant, of course. Cuddling and kissing children wasn't considered manly in his society, and men didn't do it often. So he simply looked at Al-Aqra' and said, "If you don't show mercy, mercy will not be shown toward you."[26] One meaning of this hadith is that if you don't show your affection and love, people will have trouble expressing their love and affection towards you. And we all need love and affection in our lives.

The women companions of the Prophet ṣallallāhu 'alaihi wa sallam were not limited to being stereotypical women, either. We all know that the first Muslim after the Prophet Muḥammad ṣallallāhu 'alaihi wa sallam was his wife Khadijah raḍiyallāhu'anhā.

Did you also know that the first person who bravely gave up her life defending Islam in Mecca was also a woman?

Her name was Sumayyah bint Khabbāt raḍiyallāhu'anhā. When she announced that she had become a Muslim, there were only six other people who were publicly Muslim in Mecca. Being known as a Muslim put your life at risk back then. The leaders of Mecca hated Muslims. Sumayyah didn't have a strong family who could protect her, so the Meccans captured her and tortured her, hoping she would leave Islam. But she believed that Allah would reward her for being Muslim, even if the Quraish hated it. So she bravely maintained her faith until they tortured her to death. May Allah have mercy on her.[27]

Even in Medina, women actively defended the Prophet ṣallallāhu 'alaihi wa sallam and the Muslim society against attacks from enemies. They went to the battlefield as medics and even joined the fighting, especially when things got very tough.

I'm sure you must have heard or read about the Battle of Uḥud. But I'm going to tell you a little bit about it, just in case you haven't. The Battle of Uḥud was fought between Muslims who were living in Medina and a big army of pagan disbelievers that came from Mecca. At one point during this conflict, some of the Muslims thought they had lost the battle and ran away from the battlefield.

Do you know who kept fighting alongside the Prophet ṣallallāhu ʿalaihi wa sallam and defending him even when many others were running away? A companion named Nusaibah bint Kaʿab raḍiyallāhu ʿanhā. She was one of the few companions who stood by the Messenger, **defending** him with a sword (and some say a bow as well!) until the rest of the Muslims managed to regroup and come to help.[28] The Prophet ṣallallāhu ʿalaihi wa sallam later said, "Wherever I turned, to the left or the right, I saw her fighting for me."

During peaceful times, women around the Prophet ṣallallāhu ʿalaihi wa sallam were busy learning Islam from him. They went to the mosque to pray their salah behind the Prophet ṣallallāhu ʿalaihi wa sallam in congregation. They listened to his advice. They asked him questions and he answered them. And one day, a woman asked the Prophet ṣallallāhu ʿalaihi wa sallam to make a study session for women only. That way, even the women who felt shy or couldn't come to the mosque every day because they were busy could join. He agreed. The Prophet ṣallallāhu ʿalaihi wa sallam made sure that all women had access to learning. And just like many men companions became teachers, many women among them also became teachers of Islam.

In fact, the Prophet's wife, ʿĀʾishah raḍiyallāhu ʿanhā was one of the greatest teachers of Islam among all the companions. When the Prophet ṣallallāhu ʿalaihi wa sallam was alive, she would have lengthy discussions with him about things she didn't understand.[29] After he passed away, the great leaders of Muslims, like her father Abū Bakr, ʿUmar, ʿUthmān, and ʿAli raḍiyallāhu ʿanhum would ask her questions and she would teach them what she had learned from the Prophet ṣallallāhu ʿalaihi wa sallam. Sometimes she would correct mistakes made by other companions. Sometimes she would debate with them, because she had a different opinion. Everyone respected her for her knowledge and her teaching. No one told her off for debating or correcting men.

Our mother 'A'isha *raḍiyallāhu 'anhā* also made knowledge and teaching a **tradition** among women.³⁰

Like any community, there were orphan children in Medina. This means that either one or both of their parents had passed away. 'Ā'ishah *raḍiyallāhu 'anhā* used to foster orphan girls. She took them into her home and cared for them like they were her own children. During that time, not many people learned to read or write, but 'Ā'ishah *raḍiyallāhu 'anhā* thought it was important, so her girls learned. They also learned about Islam from this incredible wife of the Prophet *ṣallallāhu 'alaihi wa sallam* and *raḍiyallāhu 'anhā*.

Some of the girls 'Ā'ishah *raḍiyallāhu 'anhā* raised and educated became famous teachers of Islam themselves. One of them was 'Amrah bint 'Abdul Rahman.³¹ She became such a famous teacher of Islam that even judges would sometimes ask her opinion before they decided things in court. *Aspiring* scholars from all the big Muslim cities of her time travelled to Medina to learn from her everything she had learned from 'Ā'ishah *raḍiyallāhu 'anhā*.

So you see, Muslim men and women didn't always fit the cultural gender stereotypes that we might have in our communities. Being a good Muslim man or woman depended on being committed to obeying Allah and serving the community, and it still does today.

Of course, some men might be stereotypically manly, and some women might be stereotypically womanly. There's nothing wrong with that, except if that stereotype is harmful. Like the stereotype that men can't be loving and affectionate, for example. Or the stereotype that women are catty or ungrateful. The Prophet *ṣallallāhu 'alaihi wa sallam* didn't approve of either of those behaviors from anyone. He sometimes even warned people that Allah would not be pleased with them if they fit into these bad stereotypes. But we see from the stories of the Prophet *ṣallallāhu 'alaihi wa sallam* and his companions that you don't have to fit into a stereotype to be a good and proper man or woman.

A Few Gendered Responsibilities

There are certain responsibilities in Islam that are assigned to certain roles connected to one's sex. These responsibilities are most often related to taking care of the family. When a man and woman get married, they become husband and wife. If they go on to have children, their family will have a mother, a father, and children. In a family like that, the husband/father must take responsibility for financially supporting the family and protecting them. And because he has to take that responsibility, he can be the person to make decisions about things that affect the family. This is called *qiwāmah*, or the **responsibility of caretaking**.[32]

But we must remember something: this doesn't mean that the husband/father shouldn't discuss important matters with the other members of the family. It also doesn't mean the man should act in an aggressive or bossy way. He absolutely may not force his decisions on his loved ones with threats or force. Instead, important decisions that affect the family should be decided after **discussing** them together. A man may understand his family's situation more than his wife does sometimes, and sometimes a woman may have knowledge that her husband doesn't have. So the couple can do things in a more reasonable and fair way if they share and consider each other's opinions. In some situations, they may want to consider the opinion of all or some of their children as well. And once they make a decision, it must be explained to all family members clearly and respectfully so they can all follow it. That is the way of responsible husbands, fathers, and family heads.

Husbands and wives should be **supportive partners** to each other. They should also be **ONE TEAM** when parenting their children, so their children will have structure and not be confused about family rules. And once a decision has been made after considering everyone's views, that decision must be respected by everyone in the family.

Another thing we should remember is that, as the Prophet *ṣallallāhu ʿalaihi wa sallam* taught us with his own behavior, the tasks of running a home are the responsibility of both the father and the mother—and later their children as well. Although earning money may be mainly the responsibility of the husband, the fact is that each family can **balance** the duties of maintaining their home in the way that fits them best—as long as one partner is not expected to do far more work than the other.

In some families, one spouse may stay home while the other spouse has a job outside the home. In this case, it may be fair that taking care of the home falls mainly on the spouse who dedicates their time to that. In other families, both spouses have jobs outside the home. This type of family might divide the housework equally between them, and maybe even take turns doing different chores each month.

If the spouse who stays home is having trouble keeping up with the home or the spouse who works is having trouble paying all the bills, the other spouse may happily pitch in. Marriage isn't about each spouse doing 50% at all times. It's about *iḥsān* and striving for excellence while cooperating and supporting one another through sadness, stress, illness, and other challenges and trials of life. So sometimes one spouse can be giving 70%, for example, and the other spouse 30%. But at other times, the tables may turn and the first spouse may need help. Then the second spouse may be giving 80%.[33]

I want to tell you about a couple who had a similar situation during the time of the Prophet Muḥammad *ṣallallāhu 'alaihi wa sallam*. The husband's name was 'Abdullāh ibn Mas'ud *raḍiyallāhu'anhu*. He was one of the first men to become Muslim in Mecca. He was brave and patient, even when people in Mecca tried to hurt him. He became one of the best teachers of Islam among the companions. But 'Abdullāh was not a rich man.

His wife, Zainab bint 'Abdullāh *raḍiyallāhu'anhā*, on the other hand *was* a rich woman. So she decided to help her husband out by spending her money to buy the things they needed for their family. 'Abdullāh was grateful, as this allowed him to concentrate on his teaching. Like we said, families work out different solutions for their needs. Sometimes the wife may be the one who makes more money, and she can choose to spend it on her family, even though it's not technically her responsibility.

One day, the Prophet *ṣallallāhu 'alaihi wa sallam* was teaching Islam to a group of women. He advised them to give charity from their money and the things they owned. Zainab asked if spending on her husband counted as charity. The Messenger of Allah *ṣallallāhu 'alaihi wa sallam* answered, "Yes, and you will receive reward for two good deeds: the reward for giving charity and the reward for going above and beyond your responsibility to be good to your family."[34]

May Allah bless us to be our own true selves with all our **quirks** and **traits** and **interests**. May He bless us to be able to fully carry out our responsibilities. May Allah make us among those who go above and beyond in taking care of our loved ones and communities.

Āmīn!

(10)
Everybody Must Go Back

If you don't mind, I'd like to tell you about my grandparents. We used to call my mother's father Bon'dappa. Even when he was old, he was very handsome and fashionable. My mom tells us that he was always a kind, gentle, and wise man. He was very well-respected in our community.

But my sharpest memory of him is sadly from the day he died. Bon'dappa passed away when I was only six years old. I remember seeing my mom crying and wondering what had brought her to tears. I was sad that my mom was sad. But I didn't quite understand what it meant when people said that Bon'dappa had died.

Now that I'm all grown up, I really wish I had gotten the chance to know him better. I pray for him daily and ask Allah to give him a place in Jannah.

We call Bon'dappa's wife Bon'damma. She is a little old woman with an easy smile, kind eyes, and soft hands. She loves to watch football matches with my brothers. But she also loves to complain that they spend too much time watching TV. I hope and pray Allah protects her and lets us love her a while longer.

My other grandfather, our Kaafaa, lived with us for much longer than Bon'dappa. *Alḥamdulillāh*, I got to know him and spend a lot of time with him. I remember spending weekends at his house. He used to tell me about our family tree. I enjoyed spending time with him because he had so many great stories to tell. But as he grew older, his body and memory became weaker. He became very sick and passed away.

I never knew my father's mother. She died when my father was a little boy. Even he barely remembers her. May Allah have mercy on them both.

As the people we love grow older, we worry about their health and, ultimately, their death. Death is a sure part of life. It comes to every living being that Allah has created. And death doesn't only come to old people. Sometimes, people die of old age. Other people die after going through a long illness. Others die in accidents. Some others are seemingly gone for no reason at all.

Innā lillāhi wa innā ilaihi rāji'ūn.
We belong to Allah and to Him we all shall return.

When those we love pass away, we will still have our memories of them. They can be sweet memories, like being told amazing stories by a grandparent. They can also be sad memories, like being upset at someone. All those memories, whether happy or sad, tell the story of you and your loved one.

Sometimes, we remember them and feel SAD. We wish they were still with us. This feeling is called "grief." We feel grief when we lose family members, friends, and even pets. No loss is too little. If you loved someone or something, it's understandable that you would be sad when you lost them. In fact, we might even feel grief when people move away or when friendships end. It's an emotion we have to accept and work through.

It can sometimes help to remember the loved ones we lose with someone else and share our memories and our feelings with them.

There was a little boy during the time of Prophet Muḥammad ṣallallāhu 'alaihi wa sallam who had a pet bird called Nughair. After being the best of friends with the little boy, sadly, Nughair became ill and died. Of course, the little boy cried for his pet bird. He was very sad. The Prophet ṣallallāhu 'alaihi wa sallam heard about his grief and would come to visit him. He would sit with him and say, "Abū 'Umair, tell me about Nughair." So the little boy would share his memories and his grief with the Prophet ṣallallāhu 'alaihi wa sallam.[35]

When we lose someone we love, we have to remember that they have finished their test in this life and returned to Allah *subḥānahu wa ta'ālā*. We can pray to Allah to accept all their good actions and give them double, triple, quadruple, or even **ten times** rewards for all their worship, kindness, and other good deeds. We can also ask Allah to forgive them for their mistakes and erase them completely. After all, we know that Allah is *al-Mujīb*—the One who answers all sincere prayers.

HEALTHY GRIEVING

Grief is a normal emotional reaction to loss. Like all other uncomfortable emotions, there is a healthy way to deal with grief. Here are some things you can do to make sure you go through grief in a safe and healthy way:

1. **Share**. Like little Abū 'Umair shared his memories of Nughair and his sadness over losing him with the Prophet *ṣallallāhu 'alaihi wa sallam*, find someone you can share your feelings with too. If you feel like you can't share your feelings with another person just yet, it may be helpful to express your grief through writing or art.

2. **Make *du'ā***. Remember that making *du'ā* is our way of sharing our feelings with Allah *subḥānahu wa ta'ālā*. Ask Allah for patience to go through this very difficult time and ask for reward for being patient. Don't forget to also ask Allah to forgive any mistakes your loved one might have made and to accept them into Jannah.

3. **Be gentle with yourself**. What you're going through is something extremely tough. Your heart and emotions will need time to recover from this. So don't try to rush yourself to "get over it." Tell me. If you had a broken bone, would you be angry at your bones for not healing faster? No? Then why would you be angry at your broken heart for not healing right away? Give your heart a little more time and give yourself some love.

4. **Stay connected**. Remember that Allah has blessed you with many people who still love you. Try your best to spend some time with them. Share how you feel with them and share with them the good memories you have of the one you've lost.

May Allah make this easy for you. *Āmīn!*

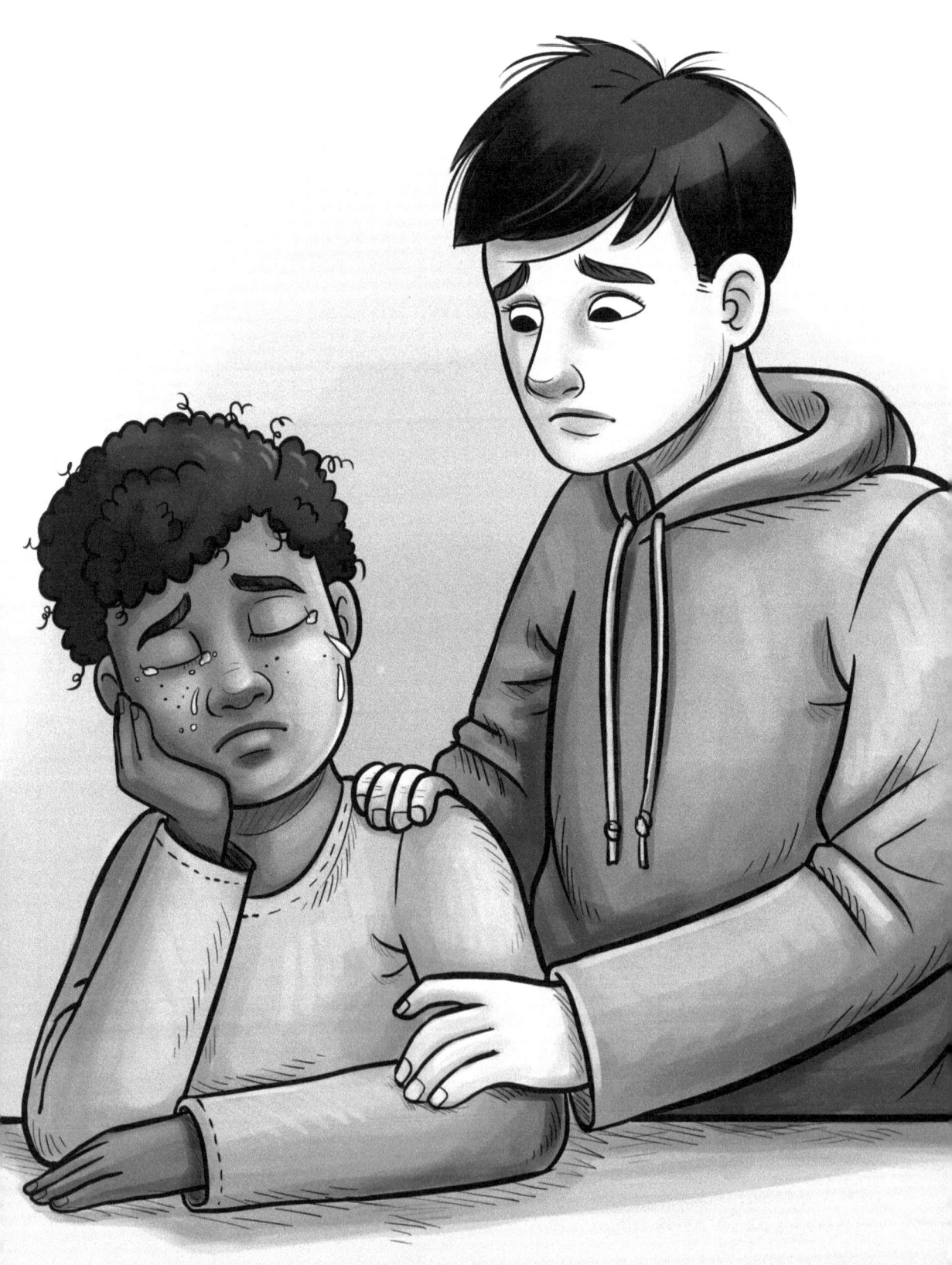

If someone we know loses a loved one, we should always remember to be gentle with them and let them grieve. We should attend the funeral prayer and make *duʿā* for their loved one together with them. We can also do a bit of chores for them. We can do their grocery run or send them a home-cooked meal. That way, they can sit with their feelings for a little while without having to worry about running errands.

And speaking of sitting with their feelings, when someone we know is grieving, we may search for "the right thing to say" to make them feel better. But making them feel better isn't always the goal. Just being with them while they feel sad is sometimes the best comfort we can give. It says, "I know you're sad and I'm here with you in your sadness. I'm not pressuring you to get over it, I'm supporting you through it."

We should also remember to let them grieve in their own way. Some people may need a little time to grieve by themselves. Some people may want to have a hug and a good cry. And people go through grief in different stages. They might not want to believe the person they love has really passed away. They might feel angry and confused. They might have trouble figuring out how life can go on without their loved one. It is important that we are kind and understanding with people who are grieving. It is also important that we don't dismiss the person's feelings. We know they can't help it. They are going through a really tough time right now, and they are just trying to figure things out.

What we can and should do is support them during this hard time. We can try to be present for them when they need us—which may sometimes be six months or a year later. Many people experience intense grief when they lose someone and seem to have "gotten over it" when suddenly, sometime later, the strong grief will return in one way or another. If this happens, we can remember to support them the same ways we did when they first lost their loved one. They will appreciate all the ways we support them, and Allah will reward us for it.

There is another thing about death that you might think of as a bit more scary. If everyone is going to die, that means **WE** are going to die, too!

A boy I know once told me that he's very scared of death. He said that he doesn't ever want to leave his parents. You see, he just loves his mom and dad so much. I think that makes perfect sense.

But we can always remember that death is actually the beginning of our trip to Allah *subḥānahu wa taʿālā*, who will reward us *inshāʾ Allāh*. Remember that in Jannah we can have our loved ones, including our parents, with us.

When we think of it that way, it can make us excited to work hard toward going to Jannah.

Our life here on earth is like a **pit stop** we make in an amazing race.[36] During this stop, we have to fuel our vehicle with prayer and good deeds. We also have to check our engine—make sure that our intentions are pure and that we do good deeds for Allah's sake, not to show off. We have to change our tires and seek Allah's forgiveness so we don't slip off the track. We should remember that we are all on the same team and try to help each other. But we also have to remember that ultimately, we alone are responsible for our own actions. Only our actions and Allah's mercy can help us make sure we properly cross the finish line.

We will definitely feel better about the race if we use this pit stop called life to prepare for the beautiful destination called Jannah. Of course, we can also choose to simply waste our time and not do any of the hard work. But that will leave us worrying about not being prepared to meet Allah.

So, let's prepare now. After that, we can trust Allah. Remember that Allah is *al-Wadūd*, the Most Loving. Allah will take care of us, our parents, our siblings, and our friends. And if we try our best and still slip up a little bit, Allah has promised to forgive us. But Allah does not accept from us to be *lazy* and to take things for granted.

So before we part ways, let us pray to Allah together one more time.

Yā Allāh! Bless us to have good and pure intentions. Bless us to do what is right and good. Bless us to do what pleases You. Protect us and our families and our friends, and give us Your Guidance. Please let us always be ready with good intentions and behavior to meet You. And allow us to be near You with the Prophet Muḥammad *ṣallallāhu ʿalaihi wa sallam* and all the other messengers and prophets and good people in Jannah.

Āmīn!

Endnotes & Additional Resources

[1] For a more in-depth read about the names and attributes of Allah, refer to the book: *Reflecting on the Names of Allah* by Ustādhā Jinan Yousef. It was published by Tertib Publishing in 2021. I think you might enjoy reading it.

[2] In the Qur'an, Allah says that He does not burden any soul with more than what that person can bear. This is in the 286th verse of Sūrah al-Baqarah.

[3] This story is narrated by Imām Muḥammad ibn Ismāʿīl al-Bukhārī in his collection of authentic hadith, which is commonly known as *Ṣaḥīḥ al-Bukhārī*. The hadith (no. 5652) is mentioned in the Book on Patience, the Chapter on the Favor Given to Those Suffering from Epilepsy. It is also narrated by Imām Muslim ibn al-Ḥajjāj in his collection of authentic hadith, which is commonly known as *Ṣaḥīḥ Muslim* (hadith no. 2570). It is narrated on the authority of ʿAbdullāh ibn al-ʿAbbās *raḍiyallāhu ʿanhu*; he once told his student, 'Atā' ibn Abū Rabāh that he's going to show him a woman who is from those who will enter Jannah, and told him to look at that tall, Black woman who is holding on to the *kiswah* (cover) of the Kaaba. Then, he told him her story.

[4] In the 23rd verse of Sūrah al-Isrā', Allah *subḥānahu wa taʿālā* commands us to treat our parents well right after commanding us to not worship anyone, or anything else.

You see, Allah created us and takes care of us. Allah also made our parents the people through whom we come to this life. So in that way, it makes sense that Allah tells us to be good to our parents as much as we can right after telling us not to worship anyone else. Our worship to Allah is an act of gratitude, and so is our good treatment of our parents.

5 Imām al-Bukhārī narrates in *Ṣaḥīḥ al-Bukhārī* on the authority of Abū Hurairah *raḍiyallāhu ʿanhu* that one day, a man came to the Messenger of Allah *ṣallallāhu ʿalaihi wa sallam* and asked, "Allah's Messenger, who is most entitled to my good companionship?" The Prophet answered, "Your mother." The man asked, "Who next?" The Prophet answered, "Your mother." The man asked, "Who next?" The Prophet answered, "Your mother." The man asked, "Who next?" This time, the Prophet answered, "Your father." This hadith (no. 5971) comes in the Book of Etiquette, Chapter on Who is Most Entitled to Good Companionship. It is also narrated by Imām Muslim in *Ṣaḥīḥ Muslim* (hadith no. 2548).

6 In the Qur'an, in the 97th verse of Sūrah al-Naḥl, Allah promises everyone who does good deeds that Allah will give them "a good life." This is regardless of whether they are male or female.

Scholars have different theories or opinions on what it means to be given "a good life." Some scholars think it might mean being given contentment. Contentment is a feeling of calmness in your heart that whatever you have in your life is just right and enough for you. Other scholars think it means that Allah will grant you happiness. Some other scholars say there is no true "good life" except the life in Jannah. So they believe this verse is a promise that Allah will give you Jannah if you do good deeds for Allah's sake. *Inshāʾ Allāh*!

7 Allah says in the beginning of Sūrah al-Tīn (from the 1st to th 4th verse): "By the fig and the olive; and the Mount of Sinai; and this safe and secure town; certainly I created the human being in the best form." Here, it's clear that the whole of the human being is created by Allah in the best form; that includes our private parts as well.

8 Imām al-Bukhārī narrates on the authority of Abū Saʿīd al-Khudrī and Abū Mūsā al-Ashʿarī *raḍiyallāhu ʿanhumā* that the Messenger of Allah *ṣallallāhu ʿalaihi wa sallam* said, "If one of you went somewhere and asked for permission to enter three times and wasn't allowed in, then that person should return."

This hadith (no. 6245) is narrated in *Ṣaḥīḥ al-Bukhārī*, the Book of Seeking Permission, Chapter on Saying *Salām* and Asking Permission Three Times. It is also narrated by Imām Muslim in *Ṣaḥīḥ Muslim* (hadith no. 2153).

9 In the 14th verse of Sūrah al-Muṭaffifīn, Allah describes the spirit and soul of those who disbelieve in Allah and says, "No; in fact, their hearts have been stained by the deeds they have been earning."

10 Once, the Prophet *ṣallallāhu 'alaihi wa sallam* saw a woman who had lost her baby during a long and hard journey. She was frantically looking for her baby son. When she found her baby, she hugged him and fed him. The Prophet *ṣallallāhu 'alaihi wa sallam* then said, "Certainly, Allah is more merciful towards His servants than this woman is towards her baby."

This story is narrated by Imām al-Bukhārī in *Ṣaḥīḥ al-Bukhārī* (hadith no. 5999), Book of Etiquette, Chapter on Having Compassion towards Your Children and Kissing and Cuddling Them. It is also narrated by Imām Muslim in *Ṣaḥīḥ Muslim* (hadith no. 2751).

11 The Prophet *ṣallallāhu 'alaihi wa sallam* liked to teach Islam to kids when they were spending happy times with him. One day, he gave 'Abdullāh ibn al-'Abbās *raḍiyallāhu 'anhu* a ride on his donkey to go somewhere. On their way, the Prophet *ṣallallāhu 'alaihi wa sallam* taught him something very important about being mindful. He said, "Be mindful of Allah; Allah will protect you. Be mindful of Allah; you will find Allah's blessings in front of you. If you ask for anything, ask from Allah. If you look for help, look for help from Allah. Remember: Even if the whole world came together to do something good for you, they can't do good for you unless it is destined to you by Allah. And even if the whole world came together to hurt you, they can't hurt you unless it is destined to you by Allah. The pens are lifted and the pages have dried."

This story is narrated by Imām Muḥammad ibn 'Īsā al-Tirmidhī in his collection of hadith, commonly known as *Sunan al-Tirmidhī* (hadith no. 2516). He studied the narration of this story historically and found that it is an authentic hadith.

12 The Messenger of Allah ṣallallāhu ʿalaihi wa sallam said: "When Muslims—or believers—do wuḍū' and wash their face, any sin they looked at will be washed away with the water—or the last drop of water. And when they wash their hands, any sin they did with their hands will be washed away with the water—or the last drop of water. And when they wash their feet, any sin they did with their feet will be washed away with the water—or the last drop of water. In the end, they will be pure and clean from any sin."

This hadith is narrated by Imām Muslim in Ṣaḥīḥ Muslim (hadith no. 244). It is important to remember that the sins Allah forgives like this are the ones that don't involve hurting other people. If you have hurt anyone, you have to also ask them to forgive you as well as asking Allah for forgiveness.

13 Allah's Messenger ṣallallāhu ʿalaihi wa sallam said: "Five things are among the actions associated with fiṭrah: circumcision, shaving off the pubic hair, removing hair from the under arms, clipping the nails, and keeping the mustache short."

This hadith is narrated by Imām al-Bukhārī in Ṣaḥīḥ al-Bukhārī (hadith no. 5889) in the Book of Dressing, Chapter on Shortening the Mustache. It is also narrated by Imām Muslim in Ṣaḥīḥ Muslim (hadith no. 257).

14 This story is narrated by Imām Abū Dāwūd Sulaimān ibn al-Ashʿath al-Sijistānī in his collection of hadith, which is known as Sunan Abī Dāwūd (hadith no. 313), on the authority of the girl herself. Another historian called Muḥammad ibn Saʿd also mentions this story as part of the biography of Umayyah bint Abū al-Ṣalt al-Ghifāriyyah; this is in his encyclopaedia of biographies, known as Ṭabaqāt Ibn Saʿd.

15 There are many stories from the life of Prophet Muḥammad ṣallallāhu ʿalaihi wa sallam where he answers questions about Islamic teachings relating to puberty, sex, and reproduction. In fact, there are so many stories that I couldn't decide which story to tell. I know you will read more and more of these stories as you grow older and learn more about Islam. They teach us that the Prophet ṣallallāhu ʿalaihi wa sallam was open, while also being respectful.

16 Many people came to learn from 'Ā'ishah *raḍiyallāhu 'anhā*, who was the wife of the Prophet *ṣallallāhu 'alaihi wa sallam* and one of the most knowledgeable scholars among the companions. One of them was a man called al-Aswad ibn Yazīd, who was from a different city. He had a young son called 'Abd al-Rahmān. Because he was a young boy, he would go and visit 'Ā'ishah *raḍiyallāhu 'anhā* even in her private room, while she wasn't dressed to go out in public. Of course, he eventually grew up and entered puberty. He came visiting to 'Ā'ishah's house and stood outside of her private room. He asked her, "Mother of the Believers, can you tell me what makes *ghusl* compulsory?" She understood that he must have begun his puberty. She also knew he wasn't married, so he wouldn't have had sex. But, she wanted to tease him a little bit and make him understand these things are natural. So, she said "Oh, if a person has sex. Have you done that, you mischievous boy?!"

This story is mentioned by Imām Muḥammad ibn Aḥmad al-Dhahabī when he talked about the biography of 'Abd al-Rahmān ibn al-Aswad in his book, *Siyar 'alām al-nubalā'*.

17 In the 30th & 31st verses of Sūrah al-Nūr, Allah says, "Say to the believing men to lower their gazes and guard their sexual desires; that is the more righteous way for them. Certainly, Allah is most well-aware of what they do. And say to the believing women to lower their gazes and guard their sexual desires."

18 Allah says in the 31st verse of Sūrah al-Nūr, "And say to the believing women to lower their gazes and guard their sexual desires; and not to show their beauty in public except the beauty that is apparent."

Scholars of Islam from the time of the companions have discussed what is the "apparent beauty" that you don't have to cover in public. Generally, all scholars agree that most of your body, except the face and hands form part of women's *'awrah*.

If you are interested in learning more, you can watch the lecture given by Ustādhā Safiya Ravat on the fiqh of women's attire and beautification. It is available in 2 parts on the Suhbah Institute website.

19 'Abdullāh ibn al-'Abbās said that the Messenger of Allah *ṣallallāhu 'alaihi wa sallam* once said, "A man should not be alone with a woman in private except in the presence of a *mahram*."

This hadith is narrated by Imām al-Bukhārī in *Ṣaḥīḥ al-Bukhārī* (hadith no. 5232). It comes in the Book of Marriage, Chapter on a Man Must Not Be Alone with a Woman in Private Except a *Maḥram* and Men Entering into the Homes of Women Who Live Alone. It is also narrated by Imām Muslim in *Ṣaḥīḥ Muslim* (hadith no. 1341).

20 Allah tells us about this son of Nūḥ *'alaihissalām* in the 42nd & 43rd verses of Sūrah Hūd. Even though Nūḥ *'alaihissalām* encouraged him to believe and obey Allah until the very end, his son refused. He died an unbeliever and was punished by Allah.

21 In the 10th verse of Sūrah al-Taḥrīm, Allah says, "Allah presents an example of those who disbelieve in the wife of Nūḥ and the wife of Lūṭ. They were married to two of My righteous servants, but they betrayed them. So they could not help them in any way with Allah, and they were told, 'Enter the Hellfire with the others who enter it.'"

22 In the 11th verse of Sūrah al-Taḥrīm, Allah presents the wife of the Pharaoh as an example for all believers. Allah says, "And Allah presents an example of those who believe in the wife of the Pharaoh, as she said, 'My Lord, build for me a home near You in Paradise, and save me from the Pharaoh and his actions and save me from the wrongdoing people.'"

23 This story is narrated by Imām Muslim in *Ṣaḥīḥ Muslim* on the authority of 'Ā'ishah *raḍiyallāhu'anhā* (hadith no. 2402).

24 This hadith is narrated by Imām al-Bukhārī in *Ṣaḥīḥ al-Bukhārī* on the authority of 'Ā'ishah *raḍiyallāhu'anhā*. It comes in the Book of *Adhān*, Chapter on the Person Who Is Busy in the Service of Their Family and when the *Iqāmah* Is Called Goes Out for Prayer (hadith no. 676).

25 This is narrated by Imām al-Bukhārī in *Ṣaḥīḥ al-Bukhārī*, Book of the Virtues of the Companions, Chapter on the Prophet *ṣallallāhu 'alaihi wa sallam* saying: If I were to have a best friend I will never part with... (hadith no. 3662). It is narrated on the authority of 'Amr ibn al-'Āṣ *raḍiyallāhu'anhu*. It is also narrated by Imām Muslim in *Ṣaḥīḥ Muslim* (hadith no. 2384).

26 Imām al-Bukhārī narrates this story in *Ṣaḥīḥ al-Bukhārī*, Book of Etiquette, Chapter on Being Merciful to Children and Kissing and Cuddling Them (hadith no. 5997). It is narrated on the authority of Abū Hurairah *raḍiyallāhu 'anhu*. It is also narrated by Imām Muslim in *Ṣaḥīḥ Muslim* (hadith no. 2318).

27 This story is mentioned by Imām al-Dhahabī when he tells the biography of 'Ammār ibn Yāsir in *Siyar 'alām al-nubalā'*. 'Ammār ibn Yāsir was the son of Sumayyah bint Khabbāt and her husband Yāsir ibn 'Āmir. Shortly after Sumayyah was killed, Yāsir was also killed for being a Muslim. May Allah accept the sacrifice and perseverance of this family.

28 The stories of Nusaibah bint Ka'b's bravery are mentioned by Imām al-Dhahabī when he tells about her biography in *Siyar 'alām al-nubalā'*.

29 One of her students, 'Abdullāh ibn Abū Mulaikah, told his students about this. He said, "If 'Ā'ishah *raḍiyallāhu 'anhā* didn't understand something, she would ask and clarify. She wouldn't stop the discussion until she understood." Then, he told the story of a time when she discussed something with Prophet Muḥammad *ṣallallāhu 'alaihi wa sallam* until she could fully understand his point. This is narrated by Imām al-Bukhārī in *Ṣaḥīḥ al-Bukhārī*, the Book of Knowledge, Chapter on the Person Who Hears Something and Asks Again Until They Understand It (hadith no. 45).

30 Dr. Tamara Gray discusses the legacy of 'Ā'ishah *raḍiyallāhu 'anhā* in her research paper that is published on the Yaqeen Institute website titled, "Courage & Commitment: The Femininity of Muslim Women."

31 Her biography is also mentioned by Imām al-Dhahabī in *Siyar 'alām al-nubalā'*.

32 In the 34th verse of Sūrah al-Nisā' Allah says, "Men have the responsibility of *qiwāmah* over women." The concept of *qiwāmah* is explained in detail by Shaikh Yahya Ibrahim in his research paper titled, "'Be a Man!' Constructing Prophetic Masculinity." You can read it on the Yaqeen Institute website.

33 The husband and wife sharing chores and helping each other in their responsibilities is part of the love and compassion they should have for each other. In the 21st verse of Sūrah al-Rūm, Allah says, "And among His signs is that He created spouses for you who are similar to you so that you can find peace with them, and put love and compassion between you..."

34 This story is narrated by Imām al-Bukhārī in the Book of Zakat, Chapter on Giving Zakat Money to the Spouse and Orphans who are Fostered in the Home (hadith no. 1466) of Ṣaḥīḥ al-Bukhārī. It is also narrated by Imām Muslim in Ṣaḥīḥ Muslim (hadith no. 1000).

35 This story is narrated by Imām al-Bukhārī in Ṣaḥīḥ al-Bukhārī (hadith no. 6203). It is in the Book of Etiquette, Chapter on Calling a Child by a Kunyah and Giving Someone a Kunyah Before Having a Child. It is also narrated by Imām Muslim in Ṣaḥīḥ Muslim (hadith no. 2150).

36 The Messenger of Allah ṣallallāhu ʿalaihi wa sallam once advised one of his companions, ʿAbdullāh ibn ʿUmar raḍiyallāhuʿanhu, and said, "Behave in this world as if you're a stranger or someone who's passing by." ʿAbdullāh ibn ʿUmar used to later advise his students to make use of this life to prepare for the life after death.

This is narrated by Imām al-Bukhārī in the Book of Softening the Heart of Ṣaḥīḥ al-Bukhārī (hadith no. 6416).

www.ingramcontent.com/pod-product-compliance
Lightning Source LLC
Chambersburg PA
CBHW042358070526

44585CB00029B/2987